DOBRO
TECHNIQUES
FOR BLUEGRASS & COUNTRY MUSIC

BY STEPHEN F. TOTH
FOREWORD BY MIKE AULDRIDGE

DEDICATION
To Louise –
My wonderful wife and best friend

THANKS:
To Mike Auldridge, Ron Middlebrook, Roger Siminoff, John Lee, Stan Jay,
and Len Stencel for their assistance and support and to Josh Graves for
his innovations and creativeness which inspired me to play the Dobro.

Cover Photo taken by Chuck Rausin at **Uncle Tom's**
119 S. Glassell St.   Orange, CA 02666

Special thanks to **Ellen Sorstokke** at Saga Musical Instruments
for the use of the Regal Dobro RD-655 for the cover photograph

SAN 683-8022
ISBN 0-931759-68-4

Published by **CENTERSTREAM** Publishing
P.O. Box 5450 Fullerton CA 92635

Contents

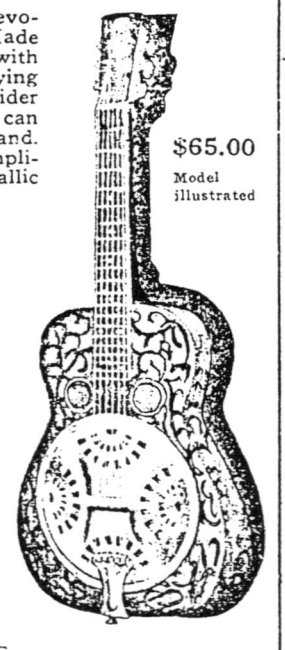

Foreword

Photo John Lee

Steve Toth has written an excellent book for the complete beginner Dobro student. The technique of explaining how to play a single - note melody, then adding harmony and finally adding rolls and fill licks to the same melody, is a very concise and clever way of getting the student to actually play something very musical in the shortest time possible. Great for getting started!

Mike Auldridge

INTRODUCTION

The dobro or dobro guitar, as it is often called, is a stringed instrument which can be played in the same manner as a standard guitar, but has become most widely known for its use when played in a manner similar to a Hawaiian guitar or steel guitar. In the years since it was introduced, the dobro guitar and the word "dobro" have become associated with several different meanings. The definitions below will acquaint you with these meanings.

The word "Dobro" is the brand name for resophonic or resonator instruments, primarily guitars, invented and introduced in the late 1920's by John Dopyera.

Over the years since the "Dobro" was introduced, the word "dobro" became associated with any resophonic or resonator type guitar. Many other brands of resonator type guitars have been produced such as: Regal Dobros made by Saga, Scheerhorn Resonator Guitars, Morrrell, Dobro by Mosrite, Sho-Bro, National, Beltona (made in England), R. E. Lee, and R. Q. Jones. Some have resonators similar to the "Dobro," while others are quite different. All types, however, have come to be referred to as a "dobro,' although, in the strict sense of the word they are not.

The word "dobro" also refers to a style of playing a guitar similar to Hawaiian guitar or steel guitar using a bar or steel to play notes and a flat pick or several fingers to pick the strings. The strings are raised well above the frets and different notes are obtained by holding the bar against the strings at various locations. The strings are picked using the right hand, by either a flat-pick or several finger picks.

In some instances the word "dobro" is used to refer to any guitar set-up with strings raised well above the frets and played in the dobro style. Although a standard guitar is technically not a dobro, many people refer to a guitar set-up to be played like a dobro, as a dobro. Any standard guitar can be played in dobro style simply by using an extension nut to raise the strings high enough above the frets so that the bar does not touch them while playing. Any standard guitar can be used as a dobro, in this manner, even one with a warped neck which can not be used for fingering. In fact, it is an excellent idea to start learning to play the dobro on a guitar you already have since you will not need to purchase another instrument. But, once you begin to play, the investment in a genuine dobro will be well worth it.

Finally, the word dobro is a word in the Slavic languages meaning "good," In fact, the name "Dobro" was originally selected by the Dopyera Brothers for their instrument because of this definition and the abbreviation of their name. DOpera BROthers.

There are many styles of playing the dobro. This book will introduce the essential styles associated with Bluegrass and Country Music. These styles are also frequently used in folk, rock, and other music forms. They can be applied to any type of music which you may wish to play.

The basic concept of this book is to teach the techniques used in playing the dobro, not merely several songs. A prior knowledge of music is not required since the book presents, in detail, the complete essentials for playing the dobro. The tablature method of notation is used throughout.

The techniques presented are the primary aspects to be learned. The songs are presented to show the various ways in which they are used. With practice, and an understanding of these techniques and how to use them, almost any song can be played dobro style. The three finger method of picking the dobro using the thumb, index finger and middle finger will be utilized. Most of the essential picking patterns will be introduced. Barring will be limited to straight barring in order to develop accurate bar positioning technique.

The techniques should be studied and learned in the order presented. although they are not all dependent on each other. The tablature explanation section should be read thoroughly and referred to frequently until a thorough understanding is achieved.

Good luck and welcome to the dobro!

Stephen F. Toth

THE DOBRO

by Sally Van Meter

When I tell people what instrument I play, all too frequently they respond, "Dobro?" Oh, you mean that guitar that sounds like it's crying in all those Roy Acuff songs?" Well, yes, that is a dobro; yet the instrument is so much more than that. Many people, musicians and non musicians alike, connect the dobro only to country music and to just one sound or style, but resophonic guitars have a unique and varied history that deserves a closer look.

In the early days, National guitars with all-metal bodies had a solid connection with blues music. Eventually National evolved and introduced a wood-bodied resophonic guitar, and both metal-and wood-bodied dobros also became very popular in Hawaiian music. There were orchestras of dobros-even instruction courses for Hawaiian music. The country dobros sound became established in the 1920s and '30s in the music of Darby and Tarleton and Jimmie Rodgers. As country music developed more of an ensemble sound, the wood-bodied dobro found a niche in providing backup "crying" fills and helping to set the mood for the songs.

During the 1940s through the late 1950s, bandleaders like Roy Acuff and bluegrass bands like Flatt and Scruggs used the sound of dobro extensively in their music, always to the enjoyment and sometimes to the amusement of their audiences; dobro players took on the role of joker, dressing in humorous outfits and providing comedy throughout the show in addition to performing their musical duties.

The classic crying trills and sweet sound of the '40s and early '50s country dobro players remained a constant until Josh Graves joined Flatt and Scruggs. Graves played not only the traditional dobro sound but also introduced a bluesy, driving sound that included rolls similar to those played on the banjo. Shot Jackson and other steel guitar players who doubled on the dobro also brought their swing and jazz influences into the music.

The next big change for the resophonic guitar coincided with a directional change in bluegrass music. Songs from the folk music revival and even from popular bands like the Beatles were finding their way into the bluegrass repertoire. Bluegrass bands would often change the tempo and phrasing of pop tunes to match the driving feel that they were accustomed to, and the dobro seemed ideally suited to playing this new style. Mike Auldridge was one of the first dobroists to embrace the new style and thus increase the tonal capacity of the dobro.

Today, the dobro holds a position of respect and recognition for its ability to fit into all kinds of music: blues, Hawaiian, bluegrass, new acoustic, Jazz, swing, country, even Irish music Say, how about dobro as the lead instrument in a Latin-style tune? No problem; it just takes an open mind.

Reprinted by permission of Acoustic Guitar, Issue #13 July / August 1992
Copyright 1992 String Letter Press Publisher - P.O. Box 767 San Anselmo, CA 94960

Scene from the Andy Griffith Show, circa 1961,
L-R: Andy Griffith, Roland White, Eric White, Clarence White, Billy Ray Lathum and LeRoy Mack

Stephen F. Toth

Stephen Toth's interest in bluegrass and country music grew from roots in the bluegrass and folk sounds of the 50's and early 60's. At the age of 16, he added the dobro to his list of performing instruments which now includes the guitar, five string banjo, pedal steel guitar and bass. The author has recently been performing on the dobro with several bluegrass and county groups in addition to doing recording work.

The presentation of techniques in this book has been developed by the author over many years of teaching the dobro, five string banjo and pedal steel. These techniques provide a sound groundwork in the theory and practice of dobro playing.

THE DOBRO® STORY

The Dobro® story starts in 1925 with John Dopyera, who owned a musical instrument repair and banjo shop in Los Angeles, California. John was approached by a musician who was in need of a louder Hawaiian steel guitar. After thinking about the problem for quite a while, he came up with the idea of using the principle of the old wind-up victrola. Why wouldn't it be possible to take this principle and apply it to an instrument? He worked on many different designs until he finally decided to use the three aluminum cone setup with a T bridge connecting them. Thus, was born the National Tri-plate resophonic guitar.

The idea of making the body of metal came from a suggestion given by John's brother Rudy. This would give a louder and brighter sound. John and Rudy set out making the first 36 completely by hand.

After gaining acceptance for the concept, they set about obtaining patents and organizing a company which would manufacture this new musical instrument. Finding limited success due to the high costs of manufacturing, John continued experimenting until he came up with a single resonator model. This model used one large cone resonator and was much more reasonable to produce. Patents were filed on this style guitar, also. This resonating system was used in the style "O," (nickle plated model with an etched Hawaiian scene) the Duolian®, (crackled lacquer finish in a gray-green color), the Triolian, (wood-grained, metal body), and the Trojan (a wood-bodied model).

Due to some disagreements with the company, John, Rudy and Ed all resigned from National in 1928. John and Rudy started work on a completely different design of mechanical amplication for stringed instruments. The new concept used an aluminum bridge which resembled a spider's web, sitting on top of a concave aluminum resonator. The patent for this design was issued in Rudy's name. The first product model guitars using this principle were marketed in 1929 under the name DOBRO.

Although the Dobyera brothers were part owners of National and full owners of Dobro, there remained bitter competition between the two companies who were manufacturing resophonic guitars. This rivalry existed until a truce was reached in 1932 and the companies merged, forming the National Dobro Corporation.

Dobro Co. was basically known for manufacturing wood-bodied guitars, and National for metal-bodied models; although Dobro manufactured a metal-bodied guitar commonly known as the "fiddle edge." This guitar was made of three types of metal: brass, aluminum and sheet metal.

Even though it was the middle of the world's worst depression, the company could not keep up with the demand for these instruments. They licensed Regal Guitars in Chicago to assist in production in 1934.

John and Rudy left the company when it moved to Chicago in 1935. Ed and Louis Dopyera took over full management at that time. John retired to his workshop where he set about developing a resophonic violin for which he was also granted a patent.

Ed left National Dobro Corporation in 1937, returning to the West Coast. Louis Dopyera continued running the company until production was stopped by World War II. National Dobro Corporation was bought out at this time by Valco, who turned the production of the company over to the manufacturing of defense materials.

Valco returned to manufacturing musical instruments after World War II ended. The only ampliphonic guitar they manufactured was called the "Resophonic," produced under the National name.

In 1958, the name DOBRO was returned to John, Rudy and Ed by their brother Louis, major owner of Valco, along with the tooling necessary to produce Dobro® resophonic guitars.

During the remaining years of the Fifties and the early years of the Sixties, Ed and Rudy started limited manufacturing of Dobro® guitars. In 1964, they licensed Ed's son, Emil and his partners to manufacture guitars using the Dobro® trademark. Due to changes which had been made in the basic construction, the two brothers no longer felt it was a product they wanted to be involved in.

After a severe financial setback, Emil and his partners, known as Dobro, Inc., sold the company interest to Mosrite of California. Mosrite produced Dobro® guitars during 1965 and 1966.

In 1967, Rudy and Ed, along with their sister, Gabriela Lazar, and their nephew, Ronald Lazar, formed a new corporation called "Original Musical Instrument Co., Inc." This company started out by manufacturing "Dopyera Bros." banjos and the "Hound Dog®." The Hound Dog® was a resophonic guitar, constructed like the original Dobro®, using the spider/resonator assembly.

Since no royalty payments had been received and Mosrite had gone bankrupt, Ed reapplied for the trademark DOBRO, which was granted by the Patent and Trademark office. The name DOBRO reappeared on guitars manufactured by O.M.I. in 1970. The company is currently producing instruments under the trademark, using the principles of both the pre-war National and Dobro resophonic systems. O.M.I. has established a precedent of re-creating these instruments as closely as possible to the original designs and patents of the Dopyera brothers.

On October 21, 1985, Chester and Mary Lizak purchased the company from Gabriela and Ron Lazar. They plan to carry on with the traditions of the company, using the original designs and patents.

## CHAPTER ONE

Dobro Parts

Basics

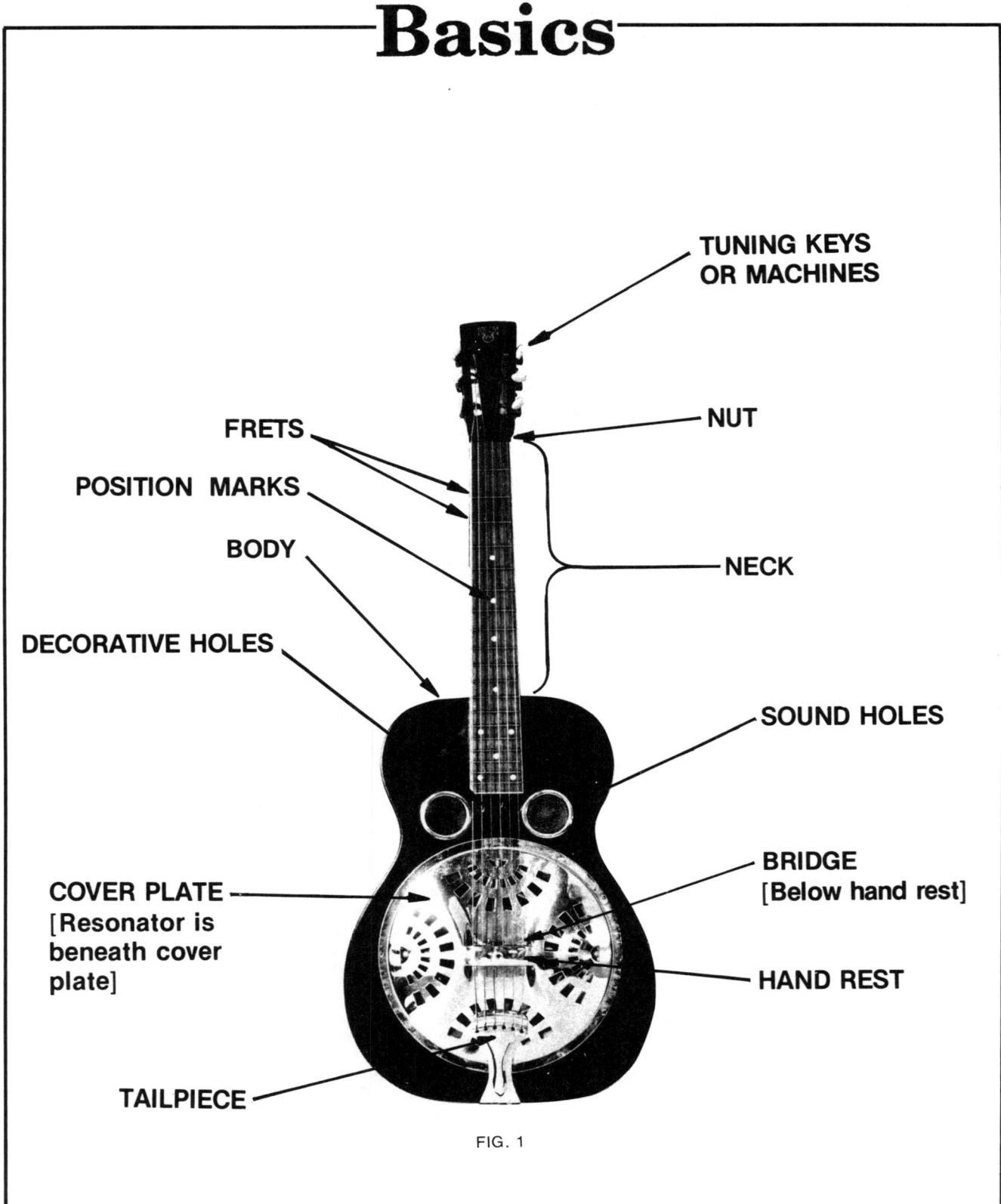

TUNING KEYS
OR MACHINES

FRETS

NUT

POSITION MARKS

BODY

NECK

DECORATIVE HOLES

SOUND HOLES

BRIDGE
[Below hand rest]

COVER PLATE
[Resonator is
beneath cover
plate]

HAND REST

TAILPIECE

FIG. 1

WORD GUIDE

Bar -
a piece of steel, plastic or other material about 3 inches long, usually rounded on at least one side, which is placed on the strings of the dobro to change the pitch of the strings played.

Barring -
the act of placing the bar on the strings.

Chord -
a group of two or more notes played at the same time.

Fill -
a note or group of notes played between the basic melody notes of a song or tune to add variety to the arrangement of the song.

Hammer-on -
a technique where the bar is rapidly placed on a string after picking the open string in order to produce another note.

Lick -
a group of notes played in addition to the basic melody notes of a song or tune. A lick is usually played rapidly, and will normally immediately precede a part of a song or immediately follow at the end of a song or part of a song.

Melody -
the basic notes of a song or tune.

Mute -
stopping the vibration of a string in order to stop a note from sounding or to eliminate unwanted sounds.

Octave -
the distance in which a musical note is repeated at a higher (or lower) pitch, for example, the distance between the 1st and 2nd "do" in "do, re, mi, fa, so, la, ti, do." An octave occurs 12 frets apart on the dobro for each note.

Open [open string] -
a string played or to be played without the bar touching the strings.

Roll -
the technique of picking the strings with the thumb, index finger and middle finger of the right hand in various patterns where no one finger picks twice in a row. Each finger normally picks a different string.

Run -
a lick which normally leads from one chord to another while playing a song.

Slide -
the technique of moving the bar up or down the neck without lifting it off the strings while allowing the strings to ring continuously.

Steel -
another term for the bar.

Tablature -
a diagram showing where the bar should be positioned on the strings, the strings to be played and the length of time which the notes played should be sounded.

Tag -
a lick which is played at the end of a song or part of a song.

Tempo -
the speed at which a song is played (that is - slow, medium, fast, etc.)

Timing -
the order and duration of the notes played.

Triplet -
three notes played in the same time in which two notes are normally played.

Vibrato -
an oscillating or warbling sound created by sliding the bar back and forth rapidly.

9

PLAYING POSITIONS

Sitting
FIG. 2

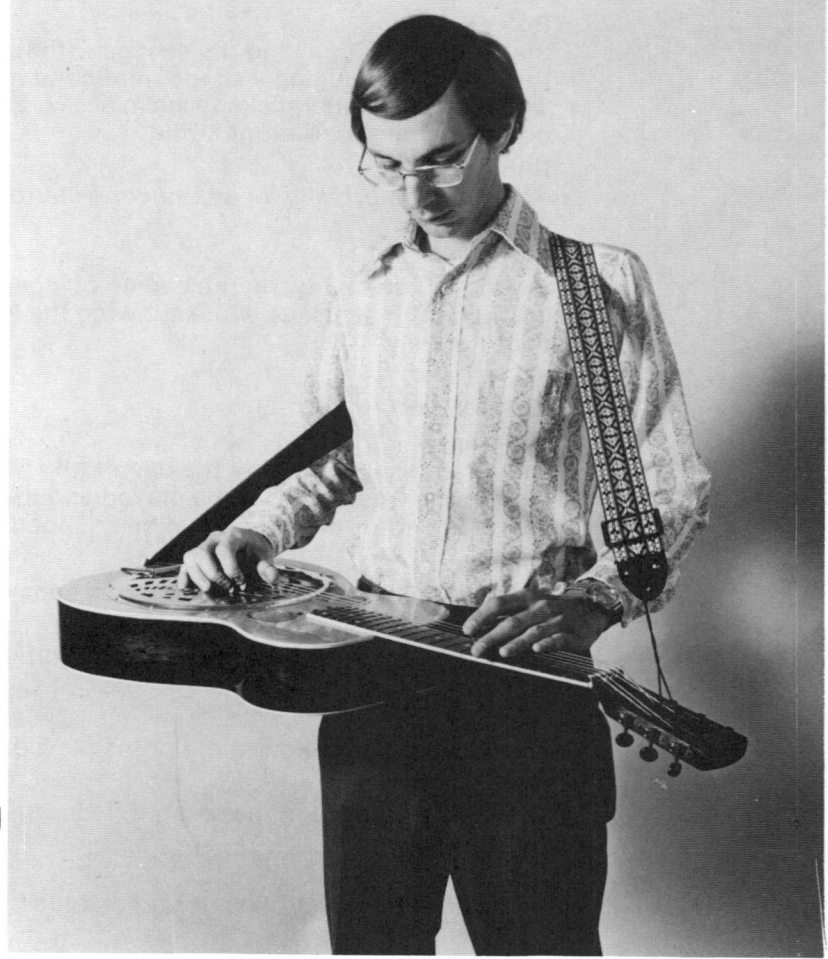

Standing
FIG. 3

TUNING

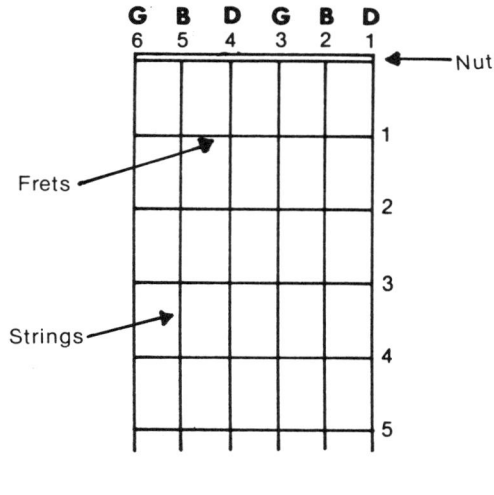

FIG. 4

There are several tunings used for the dobro. The most widely used for bluegrass and country music is the G Tuning.

Figure 4 shows the 6 strings of the dobro. Starting at the 6th string (the thickest string) the strings are tuned, G, B, D, G, B, D. Three methods of tuning the dobro are explained below.

When using a standard guitar as a dobro, medium gauge or medium-light gauge strings should be used. Heavy gauge strings are not recommended.

For a Dobro, specially gauged dobro strings for bluegrass are available.

Tuning
Method 1
Tuning To Adjacent Strings

Tune adjacent strings to each other with the bar positioned over frets as shown in Fig. 5a. Follow steps listed below.

STEP 1 -

Tune the 4th string to a standard D note using a guitar pitch pipe, piano or another instrument.

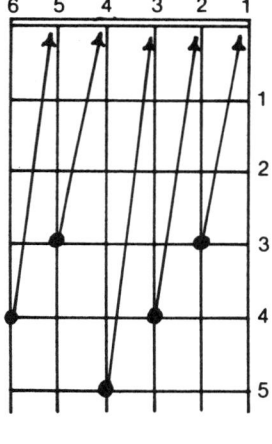

FIG. 5a

STEP 2 -

Hold the bar on the strings directly over the 5th fret leaving the 3rd string open. (Fig. 5b) Tune the 3rd string to the same sound (note) as the 4th string by tightening or loosening the 3rd string. Be careful to position the bar directly over the fret. (Note: the bar is removed while adjusting strings.)

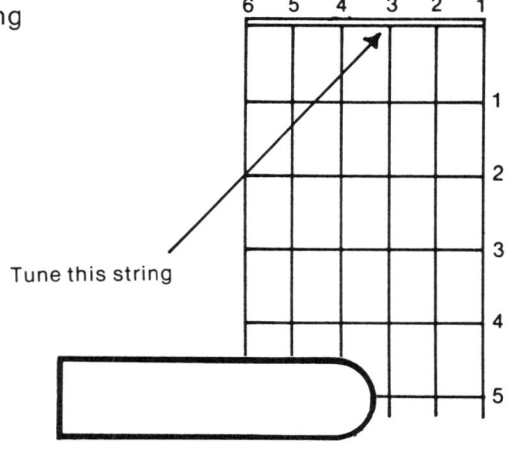

Tune this string

FIG. 5b

STEP 3 -

Hold the bar over the 4th fret leaving the 2nd string open (Fig. 6). Tune the 2nd string to the 3rd string by adjusting the 2nd string.

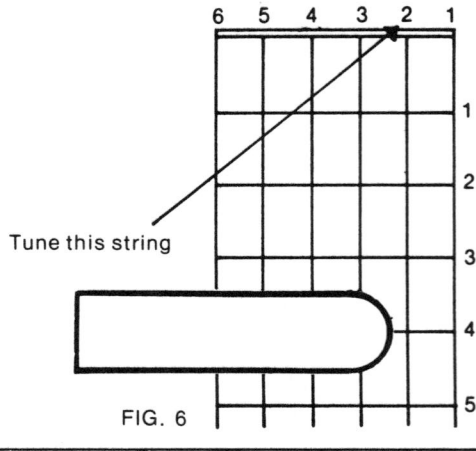

Tune this string

FIG. 6

STEP 4 -

Hold the bar over the 3rd fret leaving the 1st string open (Fig. 7). Tune the 1st string to the 2nd string by adjusting the 1st string.

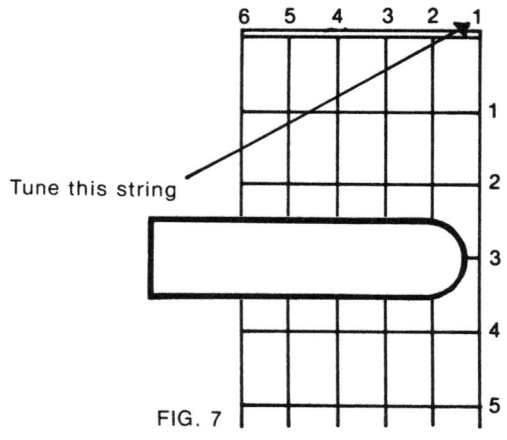

Tune this string

FIG. 7

STEP 5 -

Hold the bar over the 3rd fret leaving the 4th string open (Fig. 8). Tune the 5th string to the open 4th string by tightening or loosening the 5th string. Again, be careful to position the bar directly over the fret.

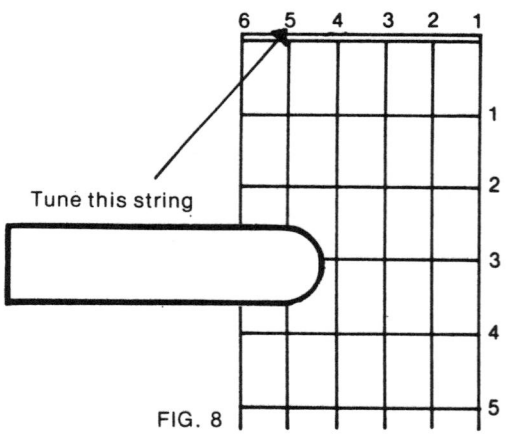

Tune this string

FIG. 8

STEP 6 -

Hold the bar over the 4th fret on the 6th string only (Fig. 9). Tune the 6th string to the open 5th string by adjusting the 6th string.

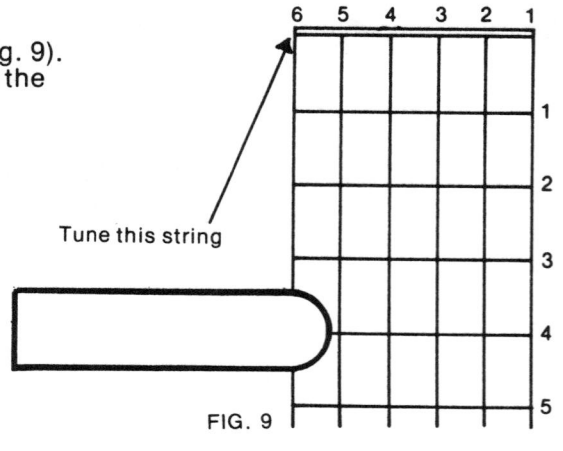

Tune this string

FIG. 9

Tuning
Method 2
Tuning To Harmonica

This method is better than Method 1. If you do not have a harmonica it is worthwhile to purchase one. This is especially true for those who do not play another instrument. An inexpensive Hohner, "Marine Band", "Blues Harp" or "Old Standby" in the Key of G will be fine.

Both the dobro and the harmonicas listed above in the Key of G are tuned to a G Chord. The first 6 notes on a G harmonica are the same as the 6 strings on the dobro. Tune each open string on the dobro to the corresponding hole on the harmonica as shown below:

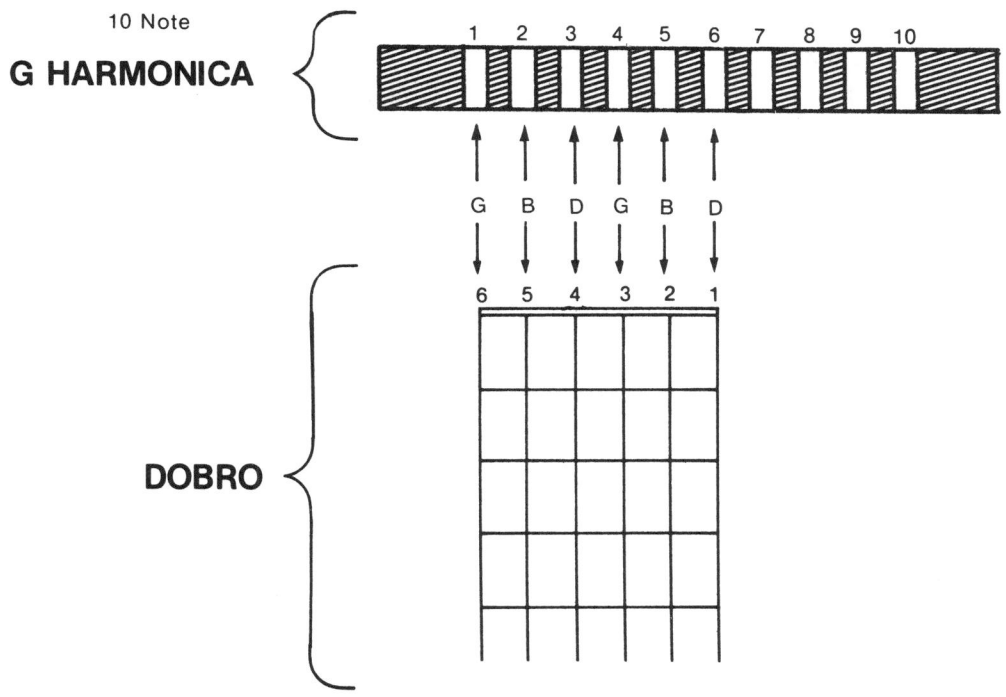

FIG. 10

John Dopyera still playing in 1986

Tuning

Method 3
Tuning By Intervals and Octaves

This method is the preferred way to tune the dobro.

NOTE:

This method should only be attempted by a musician familiar with interval and octave sounds.

STEP 1 -

Tune all strings by Method 1. This step can be eliminated once the dobro is approximately in tune.

STEP 2 -

Tune the open 1st string to the open 4th string which is the same note, one octave apart. Check this tuning with the bar at the 12th fret.

STEP 3 -

Pick the open 1st and 2nd strings. Tune this interval by adjusting the 2nd string.

STEP 4 -

Pick the open 1st and 3rd strings. Tune this interval by adjusting the 3rd strings. Check at the 12th fret.

STEP 5 -

Pick the 2nd and 3rd strings. This interval should now be in tune. If not, repeat Step 3 and Step 4.

STEP 6 -

Tune the open 5th string to the open 2nd string (octaves). Check at the 12 fret.

STEP 7 -

Tune the open 6th string to the open 3rd string (octaves). Check at 12th fret.

Tuning Hints

1. Always hold the bar directly over frets, especially when using Tuning Method 1.

2. Recheck the string initially tuned to standard pitch on a pitch pipe, piano, etc. after tuning all strings and re-tune, if required.

3. Be certain that the bar is not held slanted when checking tuning of intervals and octaves.

4. Exert even pressure on all strings with the bar at all times. This is very important while tuning and playing. Some strings offer less resistance than others and the dobro can easily be thrown out of tune while barring.

DOBRO STRINGS SETS

#3000	**JOHN PEARSE:**	Nickel wound
#1600	**GHS:**	Semi-flat, Nickel wound
J-42	**D'ADDARIO:**	Phosphor Bronze
FT13	**D'ADDARIO:**	Semi-flat, phosphor bronze
M-980	**MARTIN:**	Nickel wound

Kenny Baker and Josh Graves

A one of a kind Dobro

Scheerhorn Resonator Guitar

15

THE LEFT HAND

On the dobro the strings are raised well above the
fingerboard and frets. A bar is held on the strings by the left
hand to change the pitch of the strings and to obtain desired
notes.

Types of Bars

Many types of bars are available, but the solid steel bars shown in
Figures 11 and 12 are the most commonly used. The bar
shown in Figure 11 is probably better for the beginner since
it is somewhat easier to hold and handle than other types.

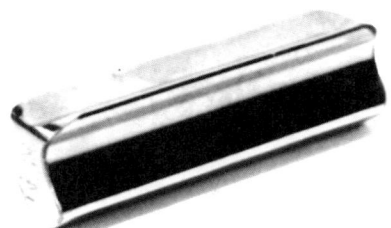

FIG. 11

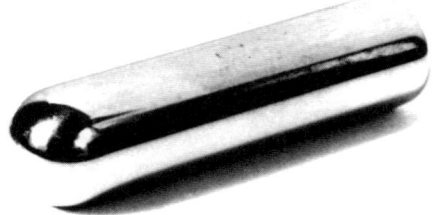

FIG. 12

Holding the Bar

The bar is held on the strings in the left hand as shown in
pictures 13a and 13b.

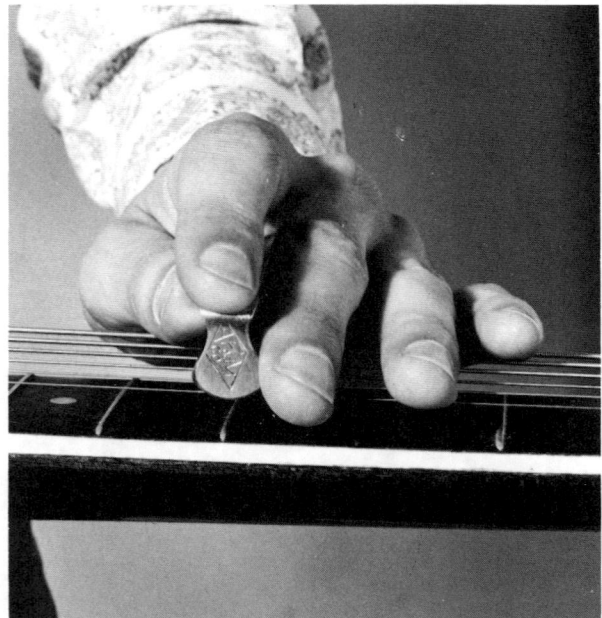

PICTURE 13a

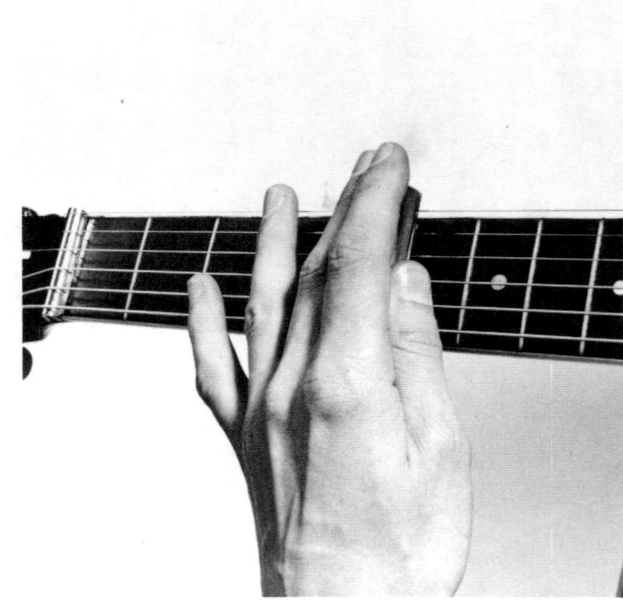

The ring finger and pinky rest on the strings to mute the strings behind the bar. The middle finger may also touch the strings at certain times. The bar should be pressed against the strings evenly with enough pressure to eliminate any rattles or buzzes. It is very important to apply pressure evenly to all strings and to keep the ring finger and pinky on the strings behind the bar.

The center of the bar should be directly over the fret being played. To check the position move head directly over the bar and center the bar on the fret. Then move head back to upright position being sure to hold the bar in same place and observe the location of the bar to the fret.

Bar Techniques

Slide

When a slide is required the bar is kept on the strings after they are picked and slid up or down the strings as called for. The ring finger and pinky also remain on the strings while sliding the bar.

Move and Mute

When a slide is not called for, the bar should be picked up off the strings and moved to the next positon. When moving the bar in this way the strings must be muted (the sound cut off) to eliminate buzzes and other noises. Moving and muting is actually a three step process:

Step 1 -

Pick the bar up off the strings about 1/2 inch with the thumb and middle finger by twisting the hand in a counter-clockwise direction. Keep the ring finger and pinky on the strings while twisting the hand (See picture 15). The string sound should then be cut off or muted by the fingers on the strings. The lifting of the bar in this way should be done as rapidly as possible.

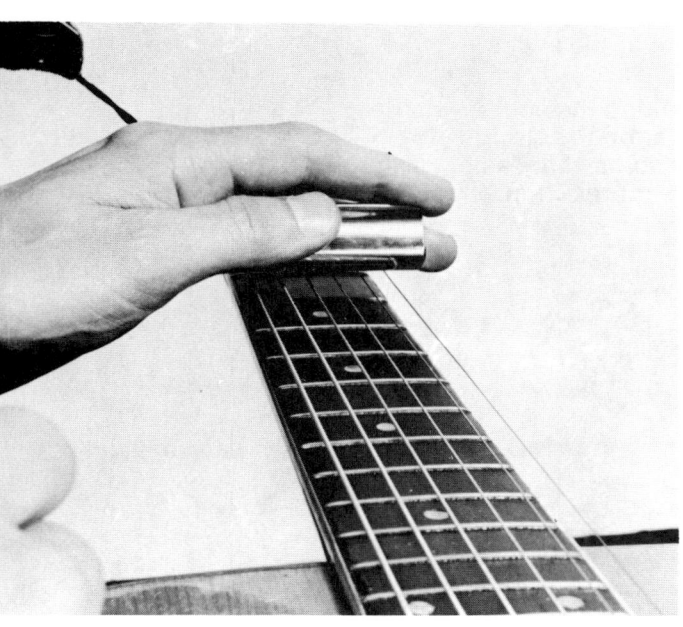

STEP 2 -

Lift the entire hand and bar off the strings. (Note: the ring finger and pinky can be left on the strings except when open strings must be played next).

STEP 3 -

Move the bar and place it on the strings at the next fret position. The ring finger and pinky should be placed on the strings before the bar if they had been removed after the previous notes played.

PICTURE 15

Vibrato

Vibrato is used on the dobro to sustain notes and vary the tone quality of notes. Vibrato is accomplished by sliding the bar slightly (about 1/8 inch) above the fret being played, then slightly below the fret being played and continuing up and down in this way in rapid succession. The bar should be held straight while sliding back and forth. (see FIG. 15).

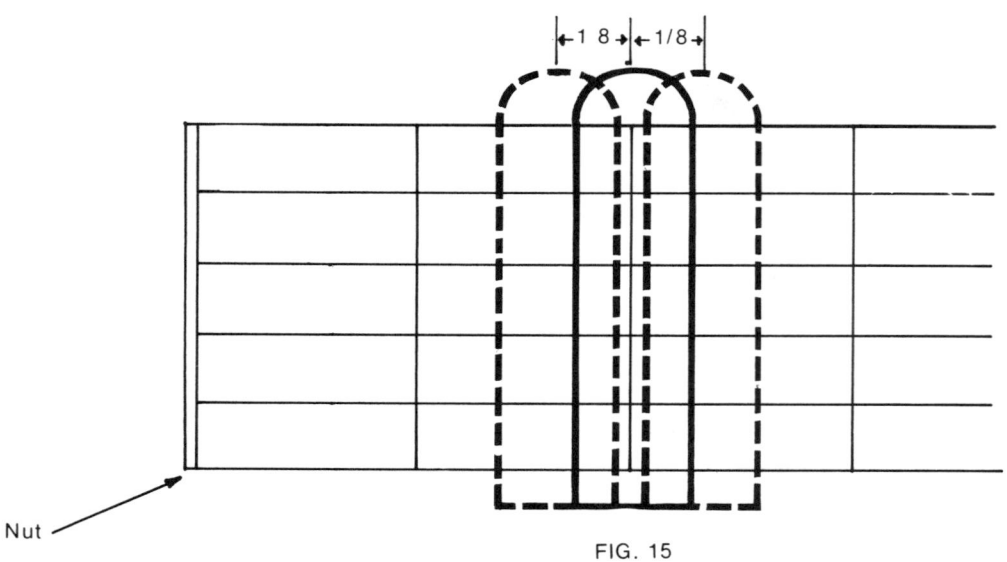

Nut

FIG. 15

The ring finger and pinky remain on the strings as the bar is slid back and forth. The bar is moved by the middle finger, index finger and thumb. The arm moves very little. The bar should always be moved an equal distance above and below the fret.

Practice slowly at first making sure that the bar is moved smoothly and that the timing and distance of the slides above and below the fret are equal.

Vibrato can also be created by rapidly shaking the entire left forearm and hand while holding the bar on the strings over the fret to be played. This method is somewhat easier to achieve, yet accurate bar positioning is more difficult than in the method described above.

Jerry Douglas

18

THE RIGHT HAND

The dobro can be picked using a flat pick, thumb pick, or thumb and finger picks. The three finger method, using the thumb, index finger and middle finger will be used in this book.

The thumb pick should be plastic. "Dobro" and "National" plastic thumb picks are good, but any plastic thumb pick can be used.

The finger picks for the index and middle fingers should be metal. "National" metal finger picks are probably the best to use.

Place the picks on the fingers as shown in Picture 16.

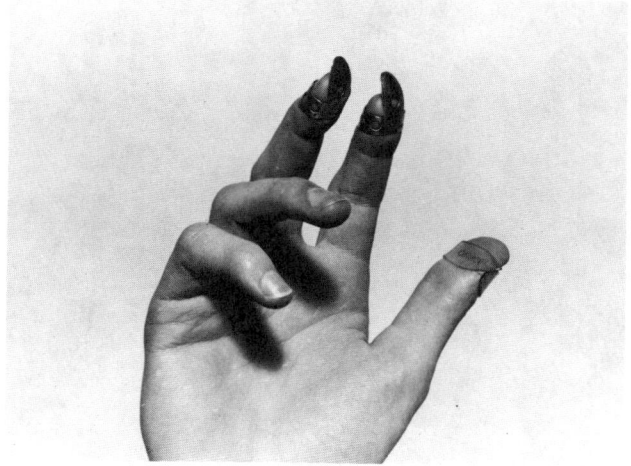

PICTURE 16

The picks should be tight on the fingers but not uncomfortable. Bend the metal picks to get them tight without pinching. It is usually not necessary to adjust the thumb pick since they are available in three sizes. If necessary, the plastic thumb pick can be adjusted by heating with hot water or steam and then bending to fit.

The right hand should be placed on the dobro as shown in Pictures 17a and 17b.

PICTURE 17a

Rest the heel of the hand and the pinky on the instrument, as shown in picture 17b. The thumb should extend out in front of the index finger. The hand and fingers should be arched as shown and should be held in a comfortable position. The hand should not be cramped although pressure is placed on the dobro with the heel of the hand to hold it from moving.

The strings should be picked with the tips of the picks. The flat face of the pick should be in line with the string. The picking hand should not be watched while playing. However, in the beginning the hand and fingers should be checked for proper position.

PICTURE 17 b

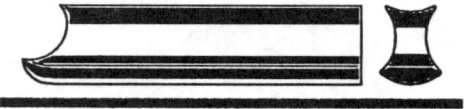

Shubb-Pearse Guitar Steel

## CHAPTER TWO

Tablature Symbols

The tablature method of instruction will be used in this book. No musical background is required. Tablature is merely a simple way to show which strings are to be picked and where the bar is to be held. The basic symbols will be explained below. Additional symbols for other techniques will be introduced and explained later in the book.

1. THE STRINGS

Each string on the dobro will be represented by a space with the string number shown in the boxes at the left of the diagram.

2. BAR LOCATION AND STRINGS PLAYED

The numbers in the space will indicate the fret over which the bar should be held and the strings to be picked. An "O" indicates that the strings are picked open without using the bar. Read the tablature from left to right.

FIRST: Hold bar at the 5th fret and pick the 2nd string.   **THEN:** Pick the open 1st and 2nd strings at the same time.

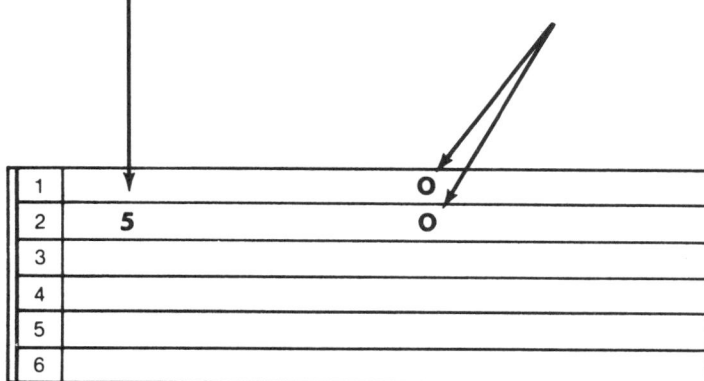

3. PICKING FINGERS-BASIC LOCATIONS

Much of dobro picking is done as follows: the middle finger picks the 1st string - The index finger picks the 2nd string - the thumb picks the 3rd , 4th , 5th or 6th string (one at a time). This will not be indicated in the tablature and should be remembered.

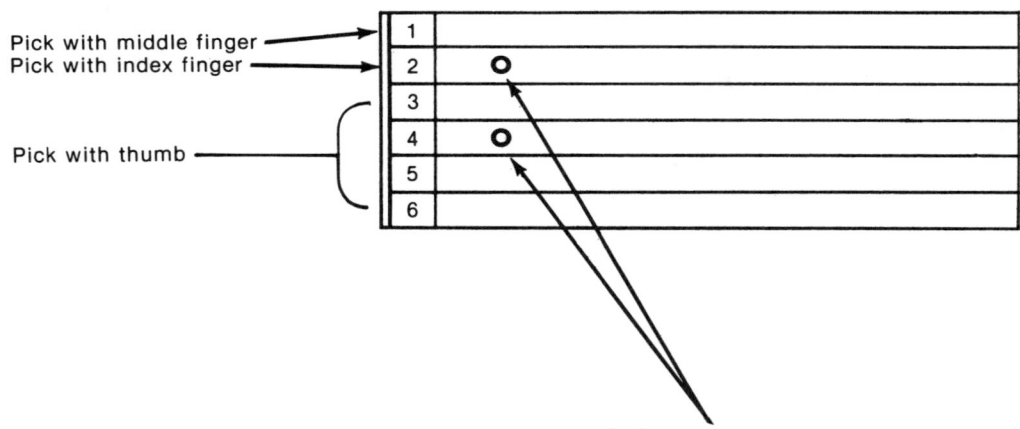

Pick with middle finger

Pick with index finger

Pick with thumb

Pick the open 2nd string with the index finger and the open 4th string with the thumb at the same time.

1st String - Basic Finger = Middle Finger

2nd String - Basic Finger = Index Finger

3, 4, 5, 6 String - Basic Finger = Thumb

Saga Regal RD-1005

22

Example 1

Try the following examples (read left to right)

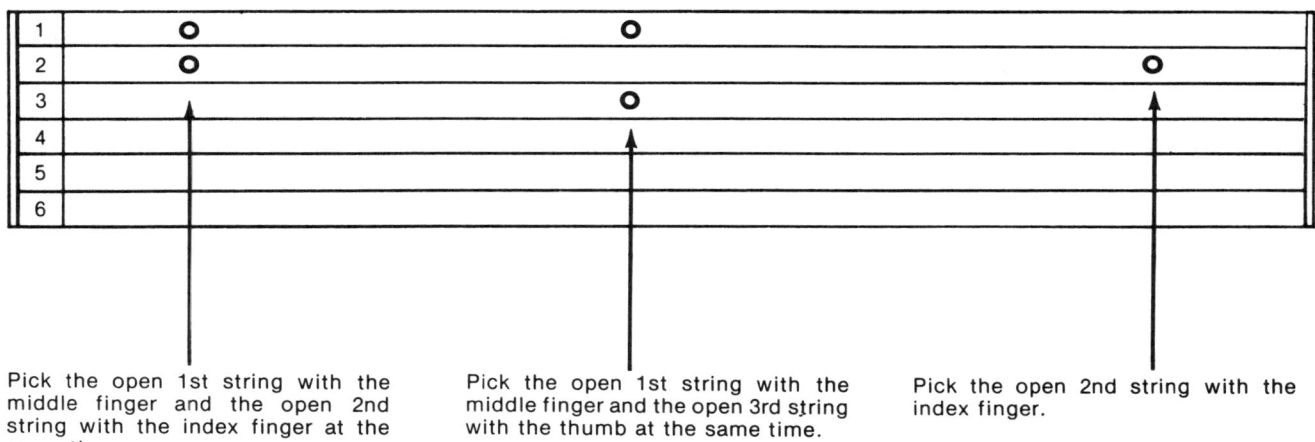

Pick the open 1st string with the middle finger and the open 2nd string with the index finger at the same time.

Pick the open 1st string with the middle finger and the open 3rd string with the thumb at the same time.

Pick the open 2nd string with the index finger.

Now play the following.

1				O							O					
2						O										O
3	O															
4							O									
5													O			
6											O					

1			O		O								O		5
2	O							O			O	5		O	5
3			O												
4	O				O					O	5				
5						O									
6															

4. PICKING FINGERS - VARIATIONS

Whenever a string should be picked by a finger different than the basic finger for that string it will be indicated by a letter as shown below:

    MIDDLE FINGER = [m]
    INDEX FINGER = [i]
    THUMB = [t]

Example 2

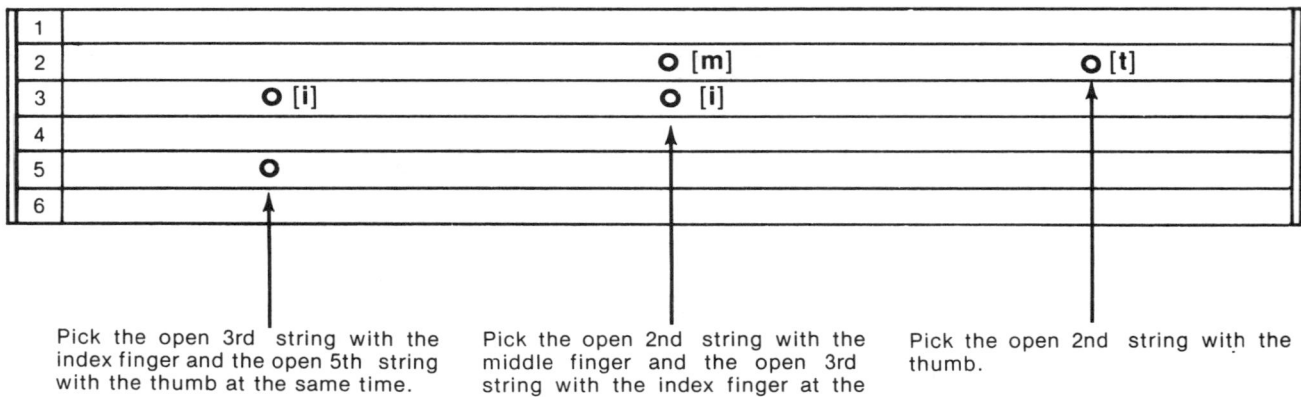

1			
2		O [m]	O [t]
3	O [i]	O [i]	
4			
5	O		
6			

Pick the open 3rd string with the index finger and the open 5th string with the thumb at the same time.

Pick the open 2nd string with the middle finger and the open 3rd string with the index finger at the same time.

Pick the open 2nd string with the thumb.

Play the following:

1		O					5	
2	O			O [m]	O	5	5	5 [m]
3	O		O [i]	O	5 [i]			5 [i]
4		O				5		
5					5			
6								

Clarence Jackson

24

5. TIMING

Timing is very important when playing the dobro. Music is divided into parts called measures. The parts are equal in length and they are separated by bar lines.

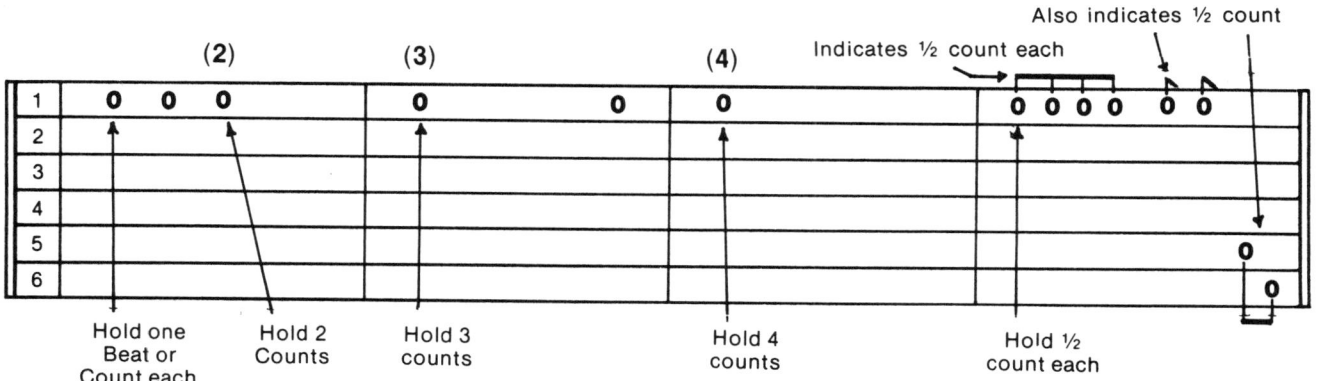

Most of the music played on the dobro has 4 beats or counts to a measure. Counting would be as follows 1, 2, 3, 4, 1, 2, 3, 4, 1, 2, 3, 4, etc. Each note which is picked can be held a different length of time or number of counts. The number of counts to hold a note will be indicated as shown below:

At certain times a pause or rest is necessary in music. This will be indicated by an R and the number of counts to rest will be indicated the same as for notes. The R will be shown in the 1st. string space for convenience, but applies to all strings.

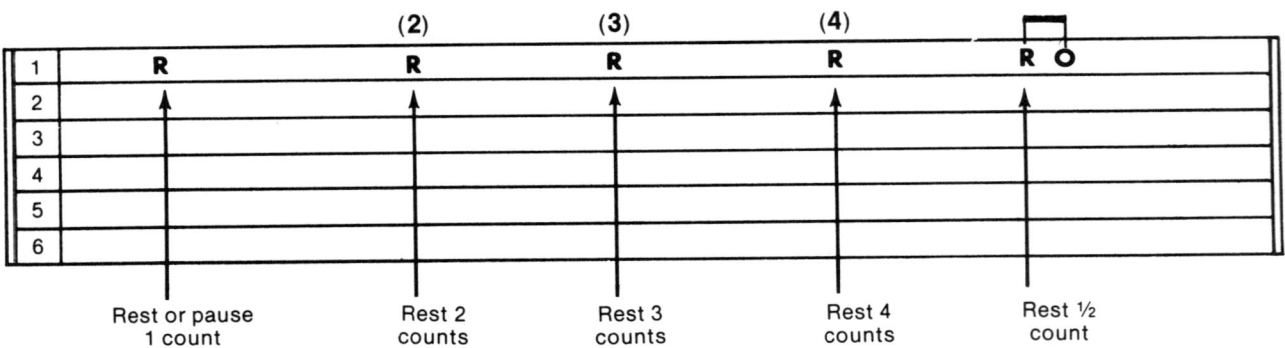

| Rest or pause 1 count | Rest 2 counts | Rest 3 counts | Rest 4 counts | Rest ½ count |

6. SLIDES

The bar is normally moved and the strings muted between notes unless a slide is called for. A slide will be indicated as shown below.

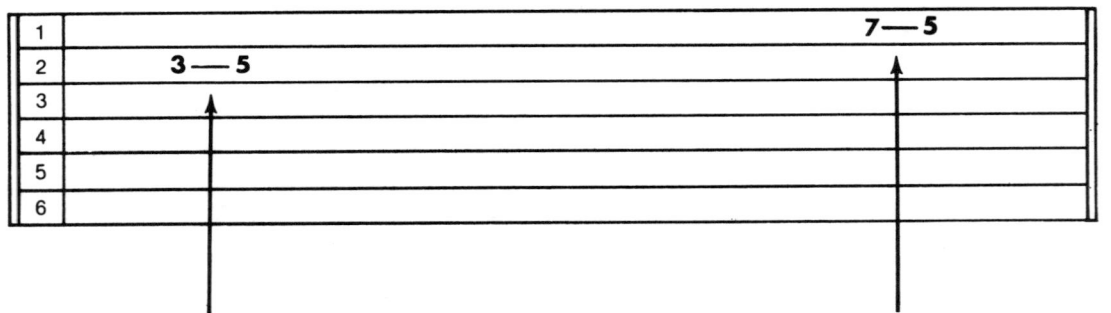

Pick the 2nd string with the bar at the 3rd fret. After picking, slide the bar up to the 5th fret, but do not pick the string again.

Pick the 1st string with the bar at the 7th fret. After picking, slide the bar down to the 5th fret but do not pick the string again.

7. ACCOMPANIMENT CHORDS

The chords to be played by instruments accompanying the dobro will be indicated directly above the tablature as shown below.

	G (2)		(2)	C		(2)	G (2)			D⁷		G (2)
1	O		O	5	5	5	O		O	O	7	7	
2													
3													O
4													
5													
6													

Brother Oswald, Ed Dopyera, and George Chestnut

27

CHAPTER THREE

Playing Techniques

There are many styles of playing the dobro. Each style has its own characteristic sounds and techniques.

For the purpose of instruction we will separate dobro playing into three styles depending on the tempo (speed) of the song to be played. These styles will be called "Slow", "Medium" and "Fast". The techniques and sounds of each are different although it is important to remember that certain elements of the three styles are often used in one song.

For each style of playing one song will be used to demonstrate the techniques to be learned. Three versions of each song will be presented. Before each version the techniques introduced in the song will be presented first with a practice exercise for each new technique. These techniques will be numbered consecutively for reference. It should be noted that the names assigned to the different techniques were selected for convenience and descriptive quality. Other names are often used in describing these techniques, yet the techniques and sounds are essentially the same.

Version #1 of each song basically contains the melody notes of the song. The melody is the actual tune which would be recognized by someone familiar with a particular song. The melody contains the notes which a singer would normally sing in a vocal arrangement of a song.

Version # 2 builds on the first version of the song. Additional notes and slides are added to the melody to obtain the distinctive dobro sound.

Version #3 contains the additonal notes, slides and fills (groups of notes) which make up a complete arrangement of a song for the dobro.

All three versions of the songs to be learned are complete in themselves and can be played as variations when playing the songs. Exercises should be mastered before attempting to play the song. When the exercise can be played with ease you are ready to play the song.

In addition to playing complete songs, the dobro is used extensively as a back-up instrument for singers or other instruments. Examples of typical back-up material are presented in the sections titled "Fills and Licks," "Introductions," "Endings," and "Chords."

MEDIUM TEMPO STYLE

Version 1 - Medium Tempo Style ————————————

Technique 1 Single note melody

Pick one string at a time as indicated in the tablature. Mute the strings when moving the bar as explained in Chapter 1 "Move and Mute". Pick strings with fingers as indicated in Tablature symbol 3 "Picking Fingers-Basic Locations."

Exercise 1

1				
2	5 5	3 5	3 5	10 5
3	5 5	5 5	5 5	10 5
4				
5				
6				

NOTE: Repeat each exercise until it can be played with ease.

Technique 2 - Timing

Tap your foot and count one number to yourself with each tap: 1, 2, 3, 4, 1, 2, 3, 4,   1, 2, 3, 4, etc. Each measure will have four counts as explained in Chapter 2 - "Timing." This is called four/four time. There are various other timings for songs but they will not be covered in this book.

Exercise 2
PART 1

			(2)	(3)	(4)
1					
2					
3	0 0 0 0	0 0 0	0	0	0
4					
5					
6					

Exercise 2

PART 2

	(2)	Rest	(2)	(3)		(4)	(2)	(2)
1	R				R			
2								
3			5	5		5	5	0
4				↑				
5								
6								

Hold for 3 counts then mute the string.

Practice Hints:

1. Try the entire song once to become familiar with the picking and bar movements required.

2. Then, start from the beginning and practice segments of the song consisting of about four measures until they can be played with ease.

3. Practice Part 1 until it can be played with ease and then go on to Part 2.

4. When you can play an entire part or song easily, practice playing it without looking at the tablature. Again, work on several measures at a time only.

Now, proceed to Version 1 of "Home Sweet Home" on the following page.

John Ely

HOME SWEET HOME (Version 1)

Part 1   Arr. S. Toth

#	(2)			C (3)		F (2)	(2)	C (4)
1	R				R			5
2			3	5			10	
3		5				10		
4								
5								
6								

#	(3)		G7 (3)		(2)	(2)	C (4)
1		5	3	2	3	O	
2	5						5
3							
4							
5							
6							

#	(2)			C (3)		F (2)	(2)	C (4)
1	R				R			5
2			3	5			10	
3		5				10		
4								
5								
6								

#	(3)		G7 (3)		(2)	(2)	C (4)
1		5	3	2	3	O	
2	5						
3							5
4							
5							
6							

31

Part 2

System 1

	C (3)		F (4)		(2)	(2)	C (4)
1	R	5	10		9	7	5
2							
3							
4							
5							
6							

System 2

	(3)		G7 (3)		(2)	(2)	C (4)
1		5	3	2	3	0	
2	5						5
3							
4							
5							
6							

System 3

	(3)		F (4)		(2)	(2)	C (4)
1	R	5	10		9	7	5
2							
3							
4							
5							
6							

System 4

	(3)		G7 (3)		(2)	(2)	C (4)
1		5	3	2	3	0	
2	5						
3							5
4							
5							
6							

Practice this before proceeding

Version 2 - Medium Tempo Style

Technique 3 Two note melody - split strings

In this technique an additional note is played at the same time as the melody note. The melody note is played on the higher string with the added note on the lower string. The string in between is skipped and not played. The picking is usually done with the thumb and index finger or the thumb and middle finger as shown in the following exercise.

Exercise 3

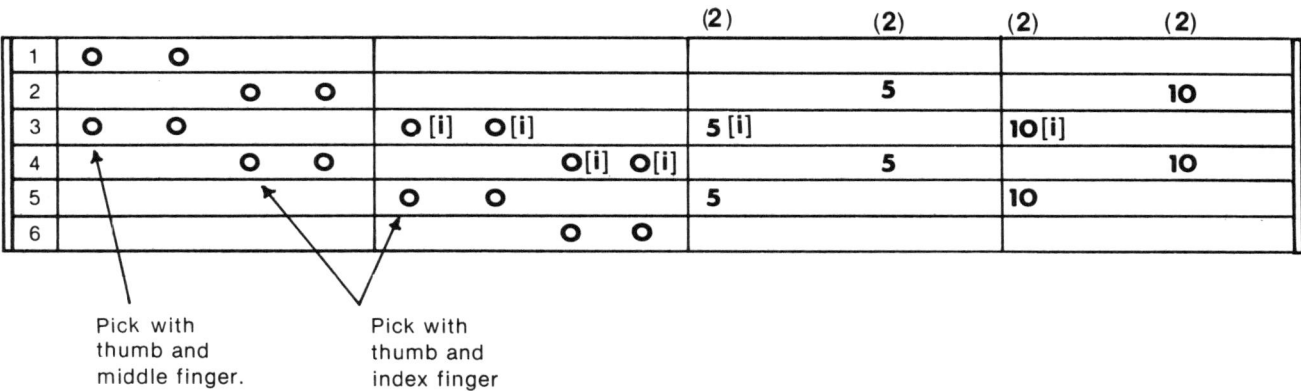

#									(2)	(2)	(2)	(2)
1	O	O										
2			O	O						5		10
3	O	O			O[i]	O[i]			5[i]		10[i]	
4			O	O			O[i]	O[i]		5		10
5					O	O			5		10	
6							O	O				

Pick with thumb and middle finger.

Pick with thumb and index finger

Technique 4 Two note melody - adjacent strings

Again an additional note is played at the same time as the melody note only this time the two strings picked are adjacent to each other. The melody note is still the higher note. The picking is usually done with the index and middle fingers.

Exercise 4

#	Part 1				(2)	(2)	Part 2							
1	0	0	3	3	5	5		3	4	5	5	4	3	
2	0	0	3	3	5	5	5[m]	3	4	5	5	4	3	5[m]
3							5[i]							5[i]
4														
5														
6														

Slides are accomplished by picking the string or strings indicated and, while allowing the strings to ring, sliding the bar to the next fret indicated. Slides can be either up the neck (that is, from a lower numbered fret to a higher numbered fret - 3 to 5) or down the neck (from a higher numbered fret to a lower numbered fret - 5 to 3).

Exercise 5

Slide bar to next fret after picking string. The bar should arrive at the next fret at the end of one count.

1	2 — 3	2 — 3	5 — 7	5 — 7	9 — 10	9 — 10	10 — 9	10 — 9
2		2 — 3						
3								
4				5 — 7		9 — 10		10 — 9
5								
6								

Pick

Do not pick hold note for one more count.

Cindy Cashdollar

HOME SWEET HOME (Version 2)

Part 1

Arr. S. Toth

	(2)	C (3)		F (2)	(2)	C (4)
1	R		R			5
2		3	5		10	
3	5[i]			10 [i]		5
4		3	5		10	
5	5			10		
6						

	(3)	G7 (3)		(2)	(2)	C (4)
1		5	3	2	3	O	
2	5		3	2	3	O	5
3						
4	5					5
5						
6						

	(2)	C (3)		F (2)	(2)	C (4)
1	R		R			5
2		3	5		10	
3	5[i]			10 [i]		5
4		3	5		10	
5	5			10		
6						

	(2)	G7 (3)		(2)	(2)	C (4)
1		5	3	2	3	0	
2	5		3	2	3	0	
3						5 [i]
4	5					
5						5
6						

35

Part 2

System 1 — Chords: C | F (3) | (2) | (2) | C (4)

String						
1	R	5——7	9—10	10——9	7	5
2						
3						
4		5——7	9—10	10——9	7	5
5						
6						

System 2 — Chords: (3) | G⁷ (3) | (2) | (2) | C (4)

String						
1		5	3	2—3	0	
2	5		3	2—3	0	5
3						
4	5					5
5						
6						

System 3 — Chords: F (3) | (2) | (2) | C (4)

String						
1	R	5——7	9—10	10——9	7	5
2						
3						
4		5——7	9—10	10——9	7	5
5						
6						

System 4 — Chords: (3) | G⁷ (3) | (2) | (2) | C | (3)

String						
1		5	3	2—3	0	5 10 R
2	5		3	2—3	0	5
3						5 [i] 5
4						
5	5					5
6						

Version 3 - Medium Tempo Style

Technique 6 Slide and Pick–Tablature Symbol 8

Tablature Symbol 8 - Slide and Pick

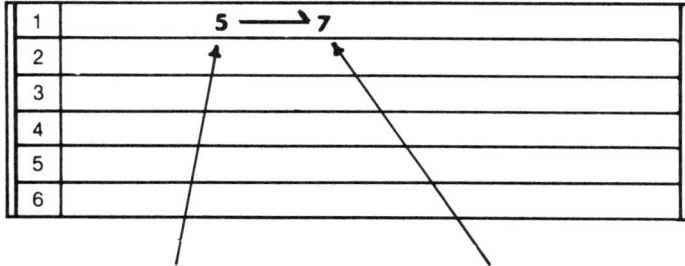

Pick the 1st string with the bar at the 5th fret. Slide the bar to the 7th fret allowing the string to ring.

Pick the 1st string again when the bar reaches the 7th fret; the slide should take the same time as the first note. In this case the slide should take 1 count or beat.

Try the following exercise and notice the different sound you get when you pick after a slide and when you do not pick.

Exercise 6

	Part 1	Part 2	Part 3	Part 4
1			R	R
2	3——5 3——⟶5	3——5 3——⟶5	3 — 4 — 5	3 —⟶ 4 —⟶5
3				
4		3—— 5 3——⟶5	3 — 4 — 5	3 —⟶4 —⟶5
5				
6				

Technique 7 Half count notes and slides

Half count notes and slides are played in 1/2 the time that a one count note is played. As you tap your foot while counting, for each tap, two half counts occur, one while the foot is going down and one while the foot is coming up. When playing half count notes it is more convenient to count 1, and, 2, and, 3, and, 4, and, 1, and , 2, and, 3, and, 4, and, 1, etc. Each "and" occurs on the up beat or upwards movement of the foot.

Part 1   Part 2   Part 3

1							2 —— 3	2–3	3		0	0	0	R	0		0	0
2	0	0 0		0	0 0													
3																		
4																		
5																		
6																		

Technique 8   Thumb-finger alternating

This is a picking pattern where the picking alternates back and forth between the thumb and either the index finger or middle finger as follows: index, thumb, middle, thumb, i, t, m, t, etc. This is a basic pattern which has many variations. The following exercise contains the basic pattern and two variations. Proper timing is essential for the variations.

Exercise 8

Part 1   Part 2

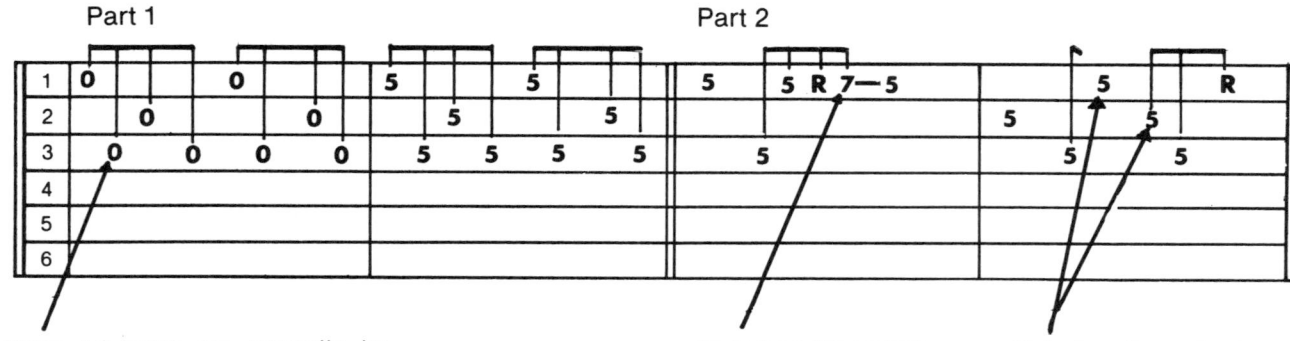

Note: All notes can normally be allowed to ring. It is only necessary to mute the strings when moving the bar.

Picked on the up-beat.   Picked on the up-beat.

Beverly King and Gene Wooten

Technique 9 Backwards Roll

This is a picking pattern where the fingers pick in order starting with the middle finger as follows: middle, index, thumb, middle, etc.

Exercise 9

Hold the tip of the bar on the 1st string at the 3rd fret and tilt the bar up in back so that the 2nd and 3rd strings are not touched.

	(2)				(2)				(2)						
1	O		O	R	O		O	R	3		3	R	3		3 2	R
2		O				O				O				O		
3			O				O				O				O O	
4																
5																
6																

HOME SWEET HOME (Version 3)

Arr. S. Toth

Part 1

C — **F** (2) — **C**

1	R R R	R 5 R	R	5 5 R 7 — 5
2	3	3 — 5 5	10	
3	5 [i]	5	9 — 10 [i]	5
4	3	3 — 5	10	
5	5		9 — 10	
6				

G⁷ — **C**

G^7 — **F** (2) — **C**

1	5 R	3 R 3 R 2	2 — 3 R 0	R 5 R
2	5 5	3 3 2	2 — 3	5 5
3	5 5			5
4				5
5				
6				

C — **F** (2) — **C**

1	R R	R 5 R	R	5 5 R 7 — 5
2	3	3 - 5 5	10	
3	5 5 [i]	5	9 — 10 [i]	5
4	3	3 — 5	10	
5	5		9 — 10	
6				

G⁷ — **C**

1	5 R	3 R 3 R 2	2 — 3 R 0	(4)
2	5 5	3 3 2	2 — 3 0	
3	5 5			5 [i]
4				
5				5
6				

Part 2

Tablature — System 1 (C / F / C)

String	C	F		C
1	R 5—7—9	9—10 R 10	10—9 R 7	4-5 5 R
2				5
3				5
4	5→7→9	9—10 10	10—9 7	5
5				
6				

Tablature — System 2 (G⁷ / C)

String		G^7		C
1	5 R	3 3 2 R	3 3 0 R	R 5
2	4-5 5	0	0	5 5
3	5 5	0 0	0 0	5
4				5
5				
6				

Tablature — System 3 (F / C)

String		F		C
1	5→7→9	9—10 R 10	10—9 R 7	4-5 5 R
2	5			5
3				5 5
4	5→7→9	9—10 10	10—9 7	
5				
6				

Tablature — System 4 (G⁷ / C)

String		G^7		C
1	5 R	3 3 2 R	3 3 0 R	
2	4-5 5	0	0	3→4-5
3	5 5	0 0	0 0	5[i] 5[i] 4 4-5
4				3→4-5
5				5 4 4-5
6				

41

FAST TEMPO STYLE

Version 1 - Fast Tempo Style

Technique 10   Single note barring - tilted bar

This technique has already been introduced in Version 3 of Home Sweet Home. However, it is widely used in the fast tempo style since much single note playing is required in this style.

The tip of the bar is placed only on the string to be picked leaving all other strings above and below open. The lower strings should be muted with the ring finger and pinky in most cases although it is not necessary to mute all of them. The string being picked is muted by the tip of the ring finger when the bar is moved. This technique should be used for almost all single note playing.

Exercise 10

Part 1   (2)   Part 2   (2)

String							
1			0				
2		0 1					
3	0 2			0 2 0 4	7 5 4		
4	0 2						
5							
6							

42

Technique 11 Up and down slide

This technique is simply the combining of a slide up and a slide down without re-picking the string at the higher fret. Remember to use the tilted bar technique for single note playing.

Exercise 11

John Dopyera, Mike Auldridge, Ron Lazar

RED RIVER BREAKDOWN (Version 1)

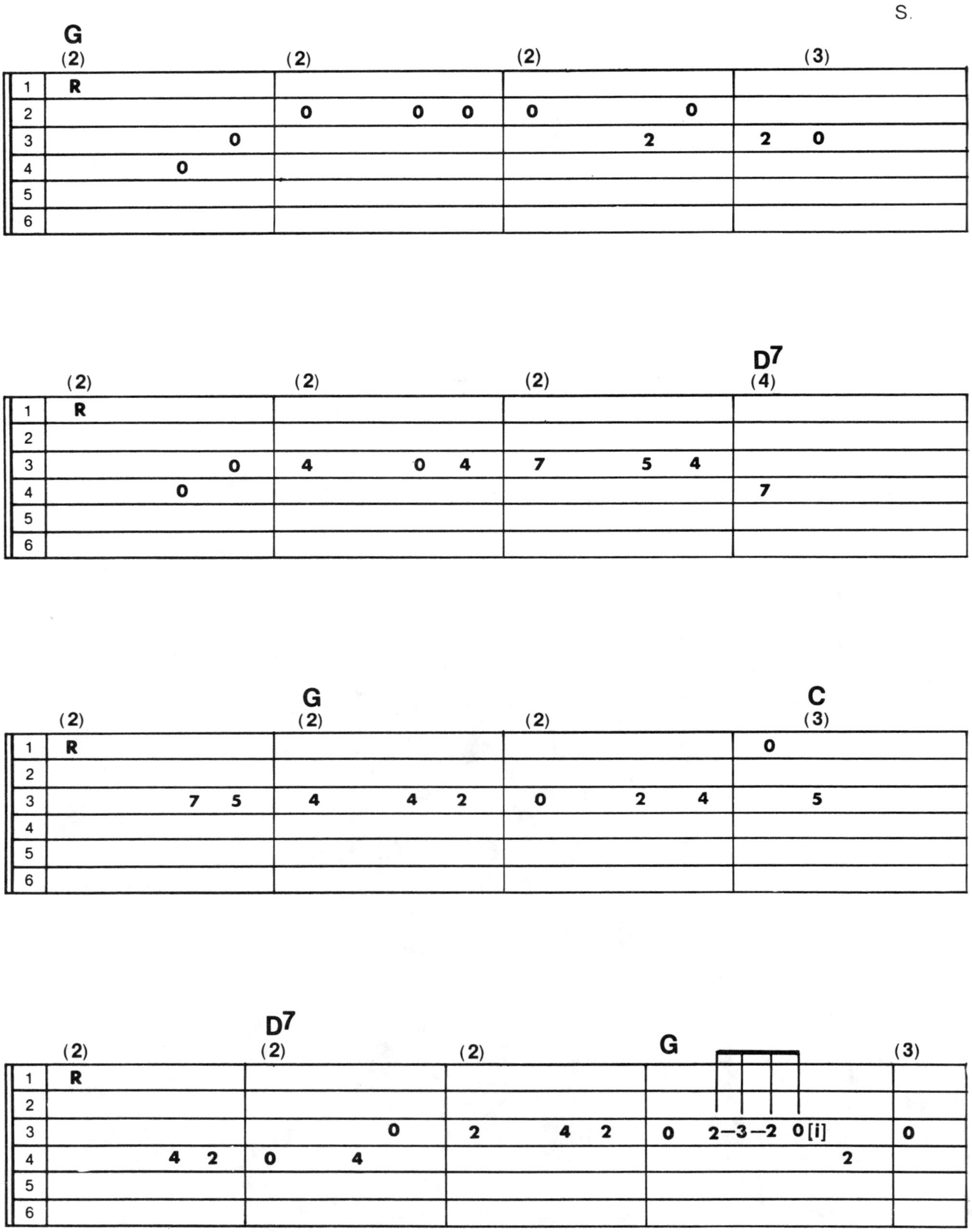

System 1 — G

	(2)	(2)	(2)	(3)
1	R			
2		0 0 0	0 0	
3	0		2	2 0
4	0			
5				
6				

System 2 — (2) (2) (2) D7 (4)

	(2)	(2)	(2)	D7 (4)
1	R			
2				
3	0	4 0 4	7 5 4	
4	0			7
5				
6				

System 3 — (2) G (2) (2) C (3)

	(2)	G (2)	(2)	C (3)
1	R			0
2				
3	7 5	4 4 2	0 2 4	5
4				
5				
6				

System 4 — (2) D7 (2) (2) G (3)

	(2)	D7 (2)	(2)	G	(3)
1	R				
2					
3		0	2 4 2	0 2—3—2 0[i]	0
4	4 2 0 4			2	
5					
6					

44

Version 2 - Fast Tempo Style

Technique 12 Pick-hold-pick

In this technique an open string is picked and allowed to ring while another string is barred and picked. The barring of the other string often includes a slide and it is important to not interfere with the sound of the first string picked while barring the other string.

Exercise 12

Part 1   Part 2

1		(2) R		(2) R		(2) R			
2	0		0					0	
3	↑ 2— 4		2— 4		0		0		2— 4
4					3 — 5		3 — 5		
5									
6									

Allow 2nd string
to ring while
playing 3rd string.

Brother Oswald

45

Technique 13 Pick-slide and hold-pick

This technique is similar to the one above. However, in this technique the string is picked with the bar on a string. A slide is then executed. When the bar reaches the end of the slide another string is picked while the initial string picked is allowed to ring.

Exercise 13

		(2)		(2)							
1		O	R	O	R	O	R	O	R	O	O R
2											
3	5 —7		5 —7		5—7		5—7		5 — 7	5—7	
4											
5											
6											

Pick the 3rd string with the bar at the 5th fret. Slide the bar to the 7th fret. When the bar reaches the 7th fret pick the open 1st string. Allow the 3rd string to ring at 7th fret.

Technique 14 Hammer-on Tablature Symbol 9

Pick an open string and rapidly place the bar on the string allowing it to continue to ring at the barred position. Care should be taken so that the string is not muted while placing the bar on the string. A hammer-on is often followed rapidly by another note picked on a different string and sometimes the same string.

Tablature Symbol 9 - Hammer-on

1	
2	
3	O ⊢——— 2
4	
5	
6	

Exercise 14

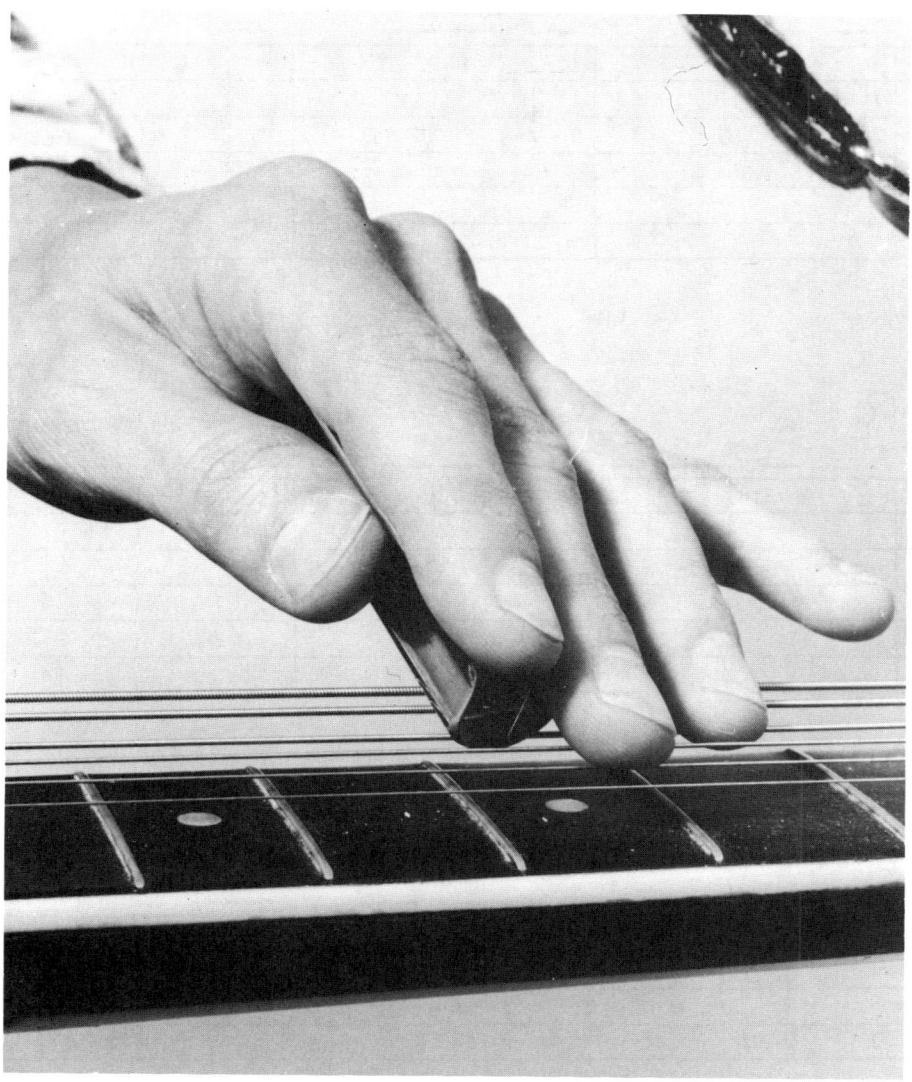

	(2)							
1	R	R	R					
2							0		0
3	0 —2		0 ⊢2		0		0	0⊢2	0⊢2
4		0⊢2		0⊢2	0⊢2			
5								
6								

Pick the open 3rd string. At the end of 1 count place the bar
rapidly at the 2nd fret allowing the string to ring

RED RIVER BREAKDOWN (Version 2)

S. Toth

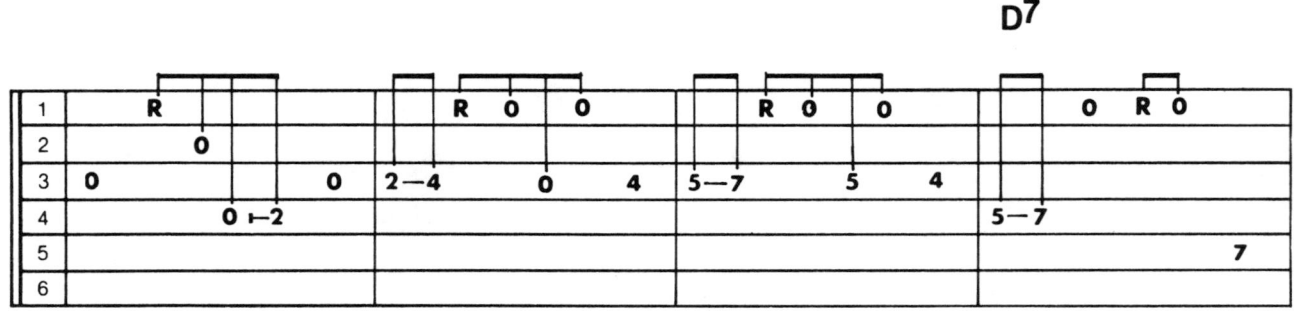

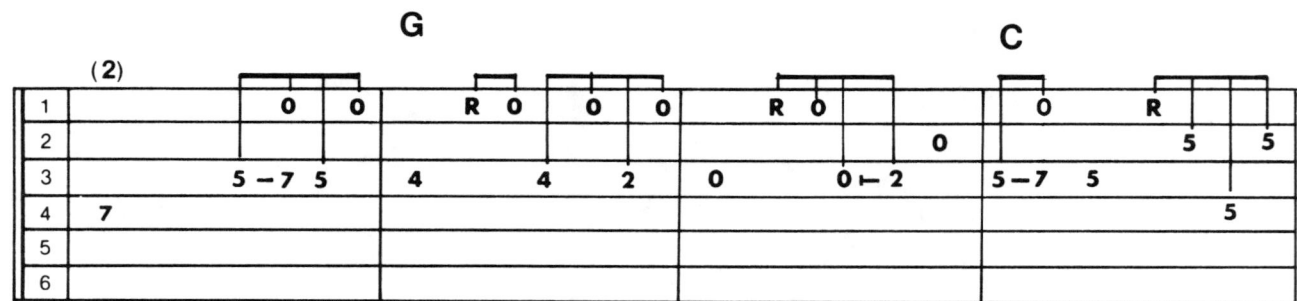

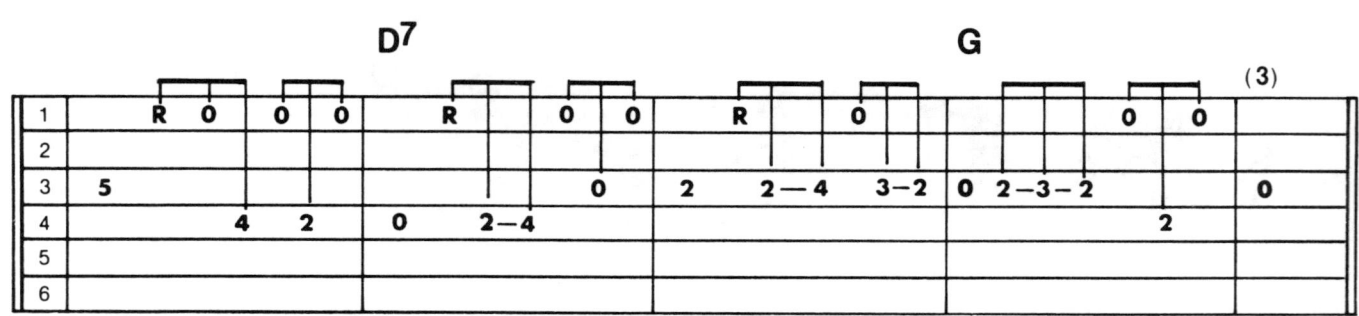

Version 3 - Fast Tempo Style

Technique 15 Forward Roll

In this picking pattern the fingers pick in order, usually starting with the thumb, as follows: Thumb, index, middle, t, i, m, t, i, etc. Each note played in the roll is normally one half count and the roll usually will be for a complete measure. Therefore, a complete roll will actually include eight notes.

The thumb will usually play the melody or lead note while the other fingers play fill notes. Most songs will contain variations on the basic pattern mentioned above as well as incomplete rolls of less than eight notes. However, once the basic forward roll is mastered the others should present no difficulty.

Exercise 15

Note: Practice rolls slowly at first until they can be played smoothly and cleanly. Place emphasis on the note played by the thumb. Gradually increase the speed of the rolls.

Part 1

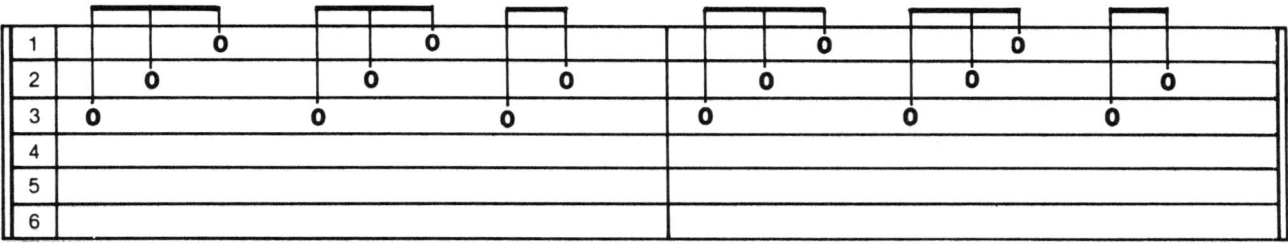

Part 2

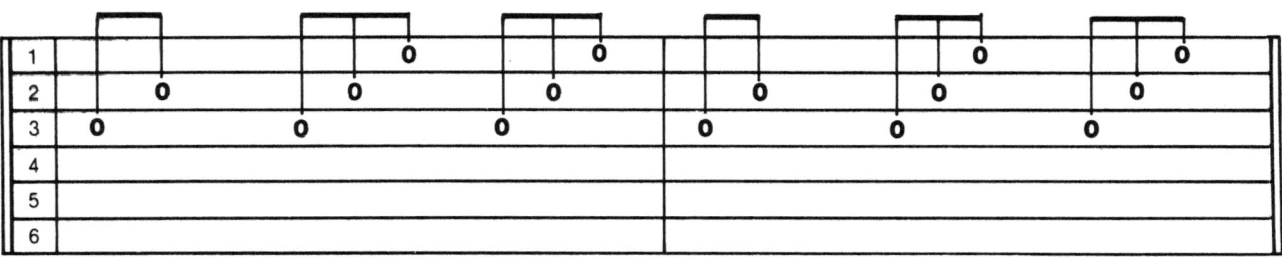

Part 3

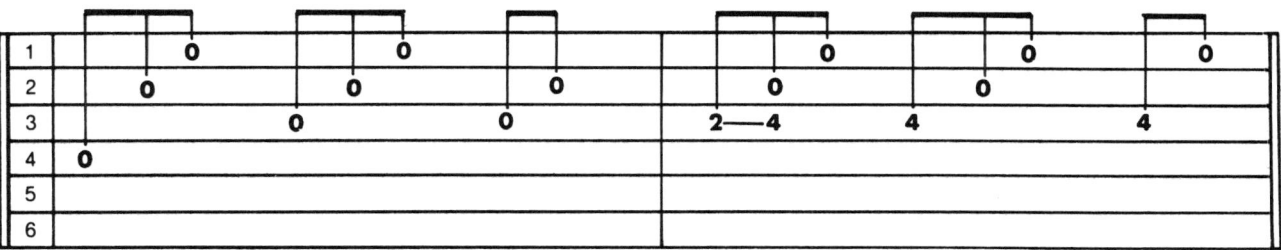

RED RIVER BREAKDOWN (Version 3)

S. Toth

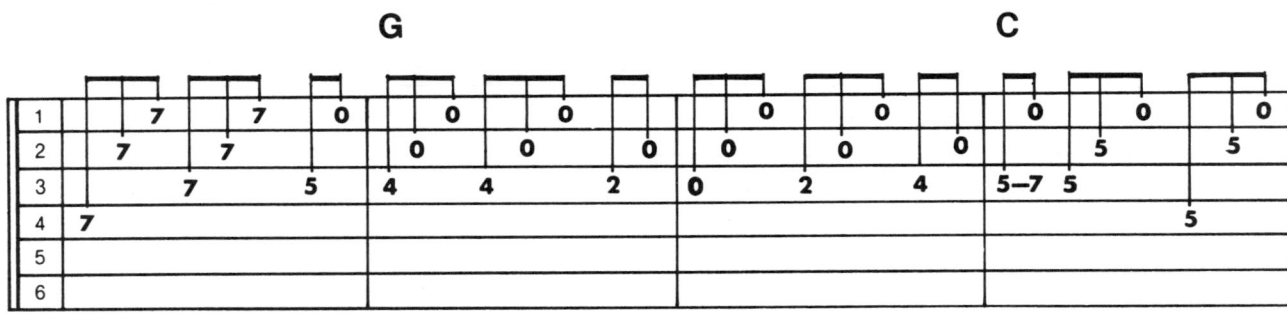

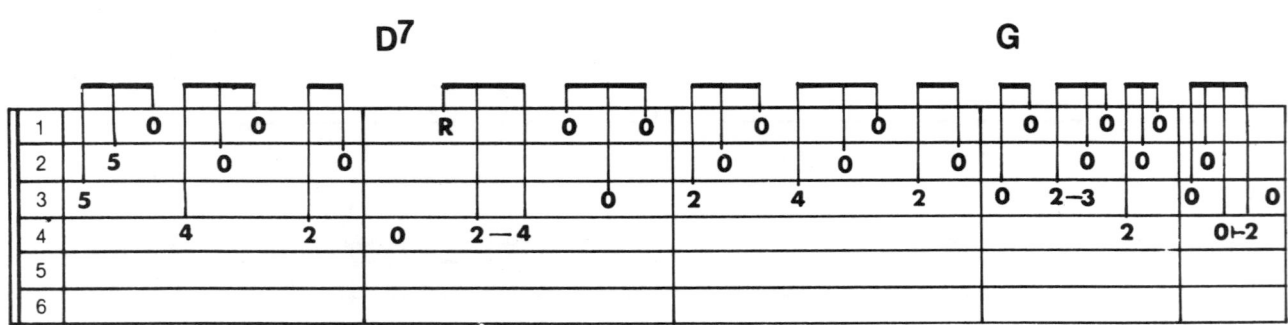

SLOW TEMPO STYLE

Version 1 - Slow Tempo Style

Technique 16 - Thumb-finger alternating thumb on 2nd string

This technique is the same as the thumb-finger pattern
learned already except that in this case the thumb moves up
to pick the 2nd string. The 1st string can be picked either by
the middle finger or the index finger. When this pattern is
repeated several times in a song the indication to pick the
2nd string with the thumb will only be shown the first time.

Exercise 16

Part 1   Part 2

1		0		0		5		5	R			3	4	5
2	0 [t]		0		5		5			5	3 [t]	4	5
3										5				
4														
5														
6														

Dan Huckabee

MAIDEN'S PRAYER (Version 1)

Arr. S. Toth

Version 2 - Slow Tempo Style

Technique 17 - Slide-stop-slide-pick

This is a combination of a slide and a slide-pick, both of which have already been learned. In the first example below, pick the 3rd string with the bar at the 5th fret. Slide the bar to the 4th fret and stop momentarily. Let the string ring and slide down to the 2nd fret and pick the string a second time.

Exercise 17

Part 1   Part 2

					(2)			(2)
1		R		R			R	
2								
3	5 — 4 —↘2		5 — 4 —↘2 5		5 —4→2 5			5 —4→2 5
4								
5								
6								

Photo John Lee

Josh Graves

MAIDEN'S PRAYER (Version 2)

Arr. S. Toth

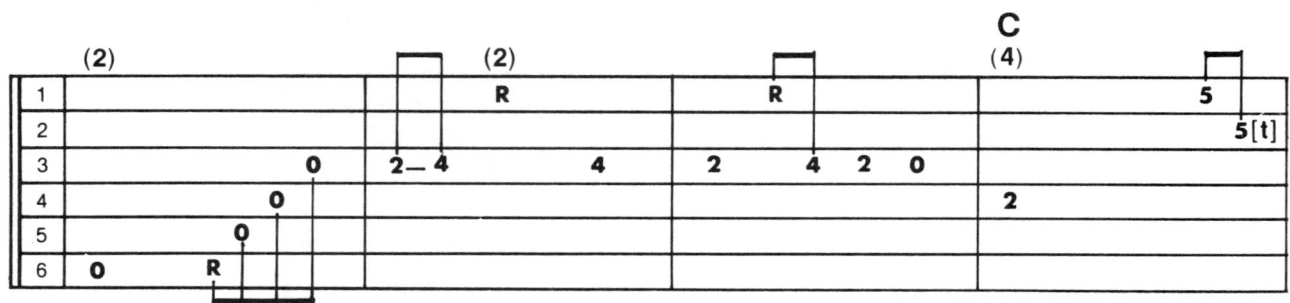

54

Version 3 - Slow Tempo Style

Technique 18   Pick two-slide one

Pick one string with the bar in position and another string open and slide the bar as indicated. Allow both strings to ring.

Exercise 18

(2)

1	**0**	**0**		**0**	**0**		**0**	**0**		**0** **0**
2										
3	**2—4** **2—4**			**4—2** **4—2**			**4 — 5** **4—2**			**0**
4										**4 — 5**
5										
6										

Technique 19   Quarter Count Notes - Tablature Symbol 10

A quarter count note is held 1/4 the time a one count note is held or 1/2 the time a half count is held. Quarter count notes usually only occur as fast slides and are similar to grace notes. A grace note is a note which precedes another note but is not emphasized.

Tablature Symbol   10

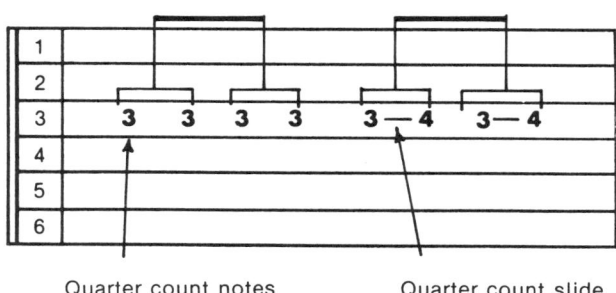

Quarter count notes   Quarter count slide

Tom Swatzell with his gold plated Dobro

Exercise 19

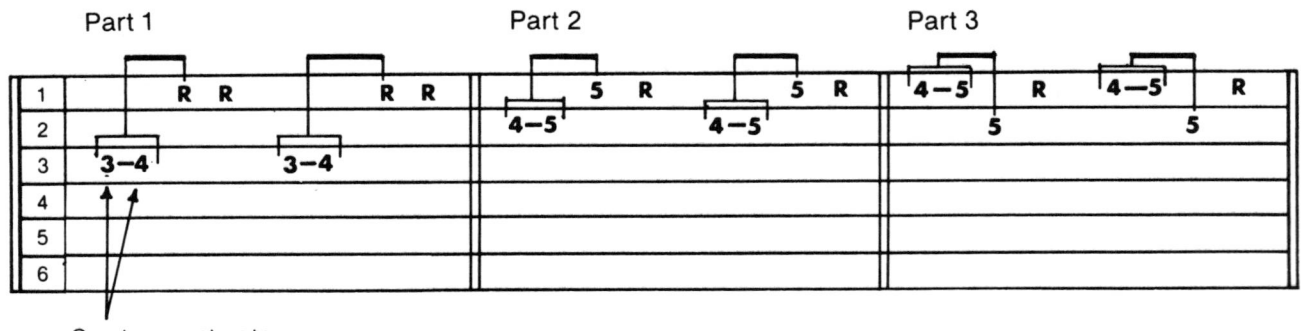

Quarter count notes

Technique 20   Quick Mute - Tablature Symbol 11

Pick the string indicated and immediately after picking,
raise the bar and mute the string with the ring finger and / or pinky

Tablature Symbol   11

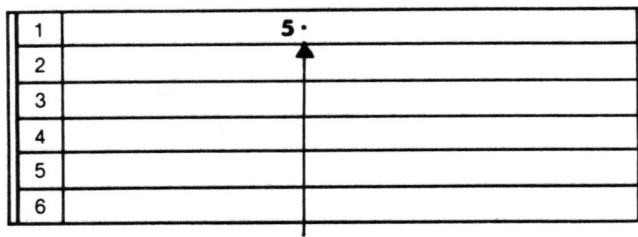

Indicates a quick mute

Exercise 20

1		5·	R		5·	R	12·		12·	5·
2	5·			5				12·	12	
3	5·			5·			12			
4										
5										
6										

56

Technique 21 Two note chords - adjacent strings

When two notes are played together on adjacent strings, the lower string is picked with the index finger and the higher string is picked with the middle finger. This should be done even when picking the lower strings. The thumb is not normally used to play two note chords on adjacent strings; although it can be done it is not preferred.

This is a variation from the basic finger locations, but will not normally be noted in the tablature from this point on.

Exercise 21

	Part 1				Part 2				Part 3				Part 4			
1	0				5		12		10	11	12					
2	0	0		0	5	5	12	12	12	10	11	12				
3		0	0	0	5		12		12							
4			0											10	11	12
5													12	10	11	12
6													12			

Use index and middle fingers

Technique 22 Triplets Tablature Symbol 12

A triplet is three notes played in the time of one count. Several triplets are normally played in sequence. The three notes are played using the thumb-finger alternating pattern with each triplet starting alternately with the thumb or a finger. All notes in a triplet take the same length of time and have the same emphasis.

Tablature Symbol 12

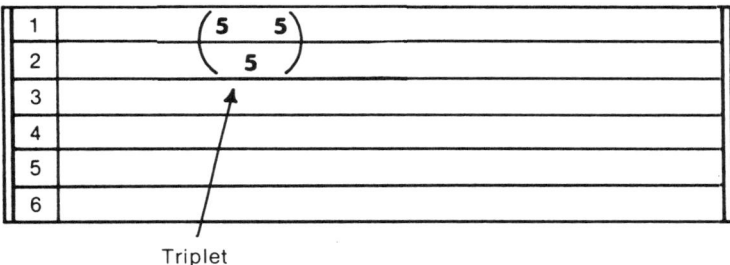

Triplet

Exercise 22

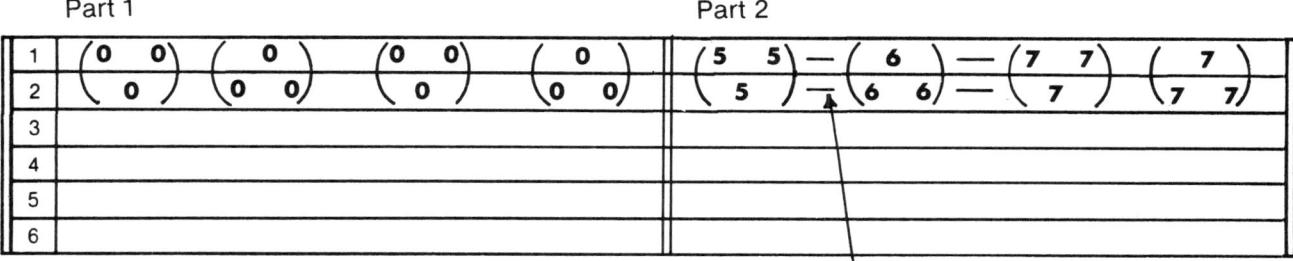

Slide to next fret while continuing to pick

Triplets are sometimes played faster than three notes to one count. The picking pattern remains basically the same however.

MAIDEN'S PRAYER (Version 3)

Arr. S. Toth

Part 1

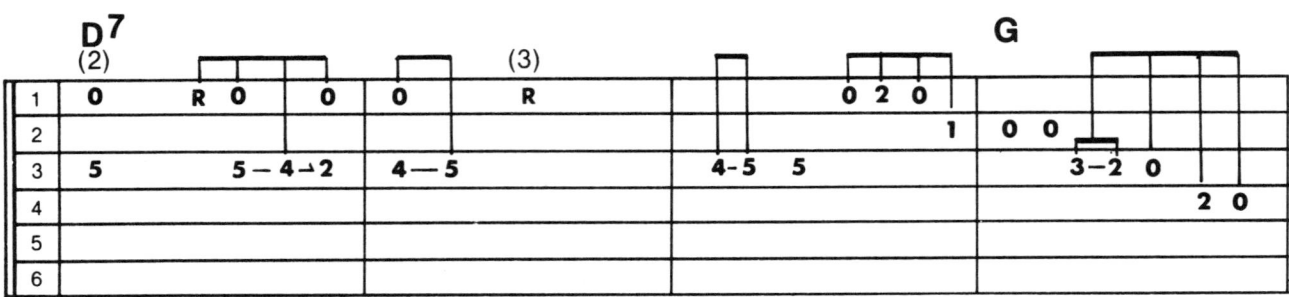

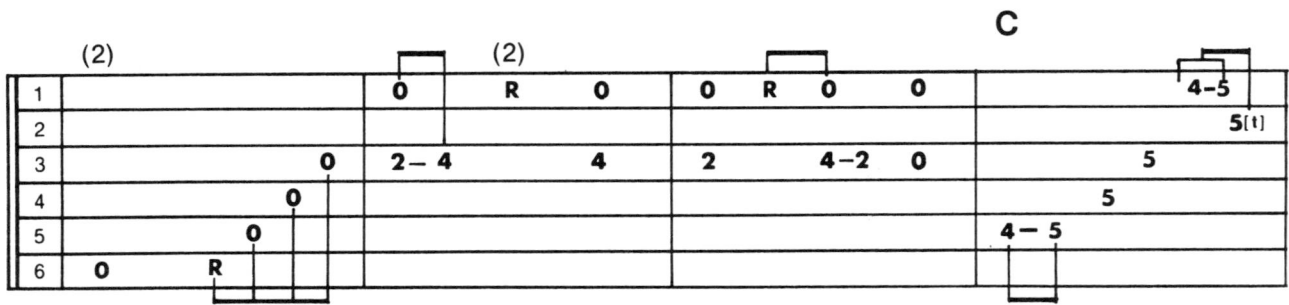

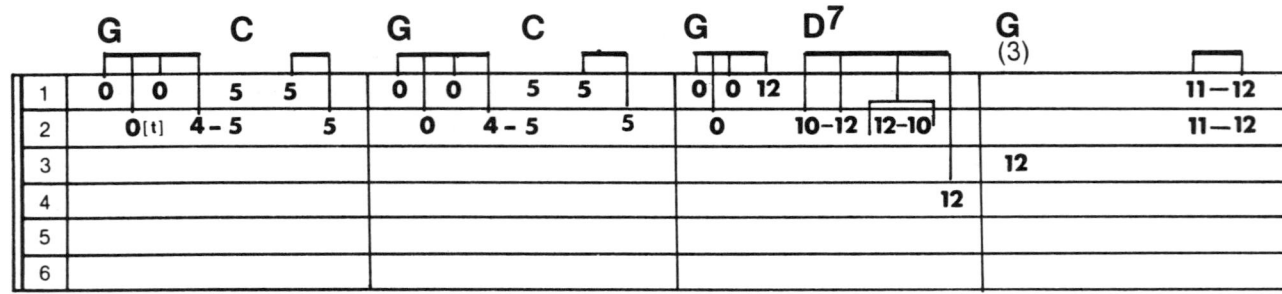

MAIDEN'S PRAYER (Version 3)

Part 2

G ... **C**

1	(3) 12	9 —10	10	R	R	5	R 5[i] 6
2	12	9 —10	10 12 [m]	(2) 12	10	12 —10 5	5 5[t] 6 7
3			12 [i]	12	10	12 —10	5
4							
5							
6							

D⁷ ... **G**

1	(7 7)(7)(7 7)—(5)	(3) 5	R 7 10 12	12 R	(2)
2	(7)(7 7)(7)—(5 5)	7	7 10	12 12 11 —12
3		7	7	12
4				
5				
6				

... **C**

1	(3) 12	9 —10	10 R R	5 5	(3) 4-5
2		9 —10	10 12 12 12	12 10 10 10 5 5	5 5[t]
3			12 12 12	12 10 10 10	5
4					
5					
6					

G **C** **G** **C** **G** **D⁷** **G**

1	0 0 5 5	0 0 5 5	0 0 12·		R
2	0[t] 4 —5 5	0 4 —5 5	0	10-12 12-10	11 11 —12
3				12	
4				12	11 11 —12
5					
6					

FILLS AND LICKS

The fills below can be used in most songs but are usually most effective in slow or medium tempo songs.

Fill #1   **Fill#2**   (3)   **Fill#3**

D   G   D

String											
1	9 7		R	R		10	11	12	R	7 – 5	R
2	7 – 5				12 10	11	12			5 – 7	
3	7			12							7
4											
5											
6											

Fill#4   **Fill#5**

D   D

String								
1	7 → 5	R	R					R
2	5 – 7			7	7			
3	7						7 [i]	
4				6 – 7	7	7 → 6 → 5		
5							5 – 7	
6								

The following licks are normally played in medium or fast tempo songs.

Lick # 1   **Lick #2**

D   (3)   G

String							
1				R	2	0	0
2							
3	0 [i]	0 [i]		0 [i]		2 – 4	0
4	0 – 2	0 – 2	0 – 2				
5							
6							

Lick #3   **Lick #4**

G   (3)   C   (3)

String								
1	5 5· R	2–3 –2 0	0	R	10 10· R	7–8 – 7 5	5	R
2			0 [t]				5 [t]	
3				0				5
4								
5								
6								

INTRODUCTIONS

Shown below are two typical introductions
which can be used to start off many songs.

KEY OF G

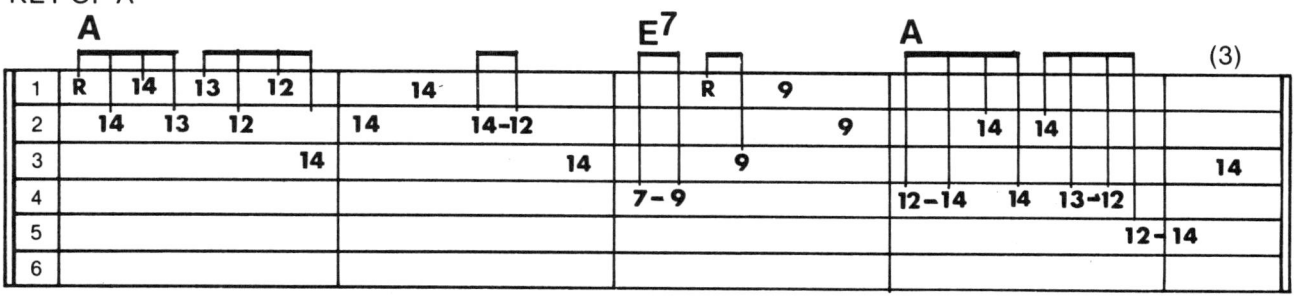

KEY OF A

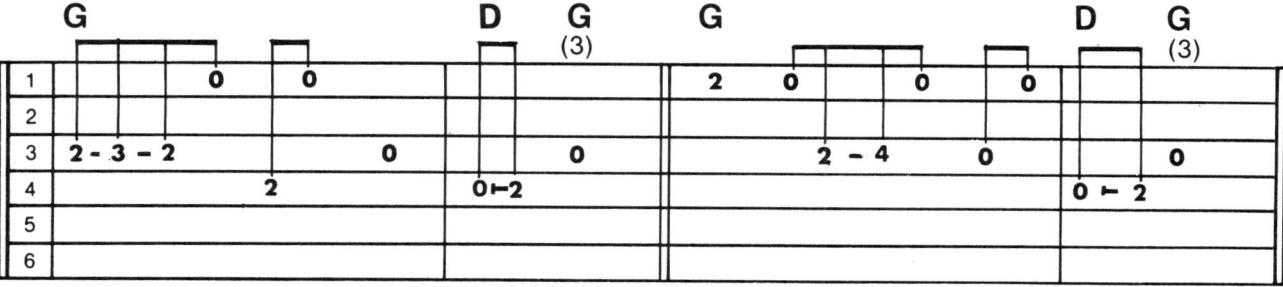

ENDINGS

Here are several endings which can be used to
end many songs. The third example is most effective for
slow and medium tempo songs.

KEY OF G - Ending #1   KEY OF G - Ending #2

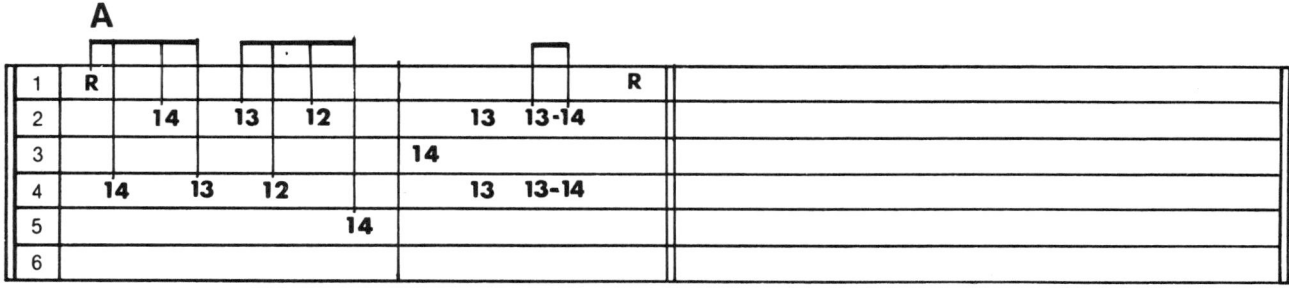

KEY OF A

CHORDS
KEYS OF G, C, B, E, F, & Bb

Each musical key has a set of chords which are used when playing in that key. Shown below are the basic chords for several of the most frequently used keys for bluegrass and country music.

The chord positions and note locations for the chords in each key are shown. The notes indicated for each chord are the notes available at one location for a specific chord. These notes are not normally played all at once, but are usually played as single notes or as various two or three note combinations. Notice that most chords can be found at more than one location.

Key of G - Basic Chords - G, C, D, Em

String	G	G	G7	C	C	D	D7	Em
1	0	12	3	5	17	7	10	2
2	0	12	3	5	17	7	10	0
3	0	12	0	5	17	7	-	0
4	0	12	3	5	17	7	10	2
5	0	12	3	5	17	7	10	0
6	0	12	0	5	17	7	-	0

Key of C - Basic Chords - C, F, G, Am

String	C	C	C7	F	G	G	G7	Am
1	5	17	8	10	0	12	3	7
2	5	17	8	10	0	12	3	5
3	5	17	-	10	0	12	0	5
4	5	17	8	10	0	12	3	7
5	5	17	8	10	0	12	3	5
6	5	17	-	10	0	12	0	5

Key of B - Basic Chords - B, E, F#, G#m

String	B	B	B7	E	F#	F#7	G#m	G#m
1	4	16	7	9	11	14	1	6
2	4	16	7	9	11	14	0	4
3	4	16	4	9	11	11	1	4
4	4	16	7	9	11	14	1	6
5	4	16	7	9	11	14	0	4
6	4	16	4	9	11	11	1	4

Key of E - Basic Chords - E, A, B, C#m

String	E	E7	E7	A	A	B	B7	C#m
1	9	12	0	2	14	4	7	12
2	9	12	9	2	14	4	7	9
3	9	9	9	2	14	4	4	9
4	9	12	0	2	14	4	7	12
5	9	12	9	2	14	4	7	9
6	9	9	9	2	14	4	4	9

Key of F - Basic Chords - F, Bb, C, Dm

String	F	F7	Bb	Bb	C	C7	Dm	Dm
1	10	13	3	15	5	8	7	13
2	10	13	3	15	5	8	6	10
3	10	10	3	15	5	5	7	10
4	10	13	3	15	5	8	7	13
5	10	13	3	15	5	8	6	10
6	10	10	3	15	5	5	7	10

Key of Bb - Basic Chords - Bb, Eb, F, Gm

String	Bb	Bb7	Bb	Eb	F	F7	Gm	Gm
1	3	6	15	8	10	13	6	12
2	3	6	15	8	10	13	3	11
3	3	3	15	8	10	10	3	12
4	3	6	15	8	10	13	6	12
5	3	6	15	8	10	13	3	11
6	3	3	15	8	10	10	3	12